It's Time

to Stop Rehearsing What We Believe and Start Looking at What Difference It Makes

Reinder Bruinsma

a sycamore tree book
from
Pacific Press® Publishing Association
Nampa, Idaho
Oshawa, Ontario, Canada

Dedication

This book is dedicated to a few men whom I have come to respect as role models: Bert B. Beach, Jon L. Dybdahl, Sakae Kubo, and Jan Paulsen.

Edited by Kenneth R. Wade
Designed by Michelle C. Petz
Cover photo Copyright © 1997 by PhotoDisc, Inc.

Copyright © 1998 by
Pacific Press® Publishing Association
Printed in the United States of America
All Rights Reserved

Library of Congress Cataloging-in-Publication Data:

Bruinsma, Reinder.
　　It's time to stop rehearsing what we believe and start looking at what
　difference it makes / Reinder Bruinsma
　　　　p.　cm.
　　ISBN 0-8163-1401-2 (pbk. : alk. paper)
　　1. Seventh-day Adventists—Doctrines.　2. Christian life—Seventh-day
　Adventist authors.　I. Title.
　BX6154.B77　1998
　230'.6732—dc21　　　　　　　　　　　　　　　　　　　97–22394
　　　　　　　　　　　　　　　　　　　　　　　　　　　　　　CIP

ISBN 0-8163-1401-2

98 99 00 01 02 • 5 4 3 2 1

 Contents

Introduction: The Truth Will Set Us Free
....5

Chapter 1: I Nearly Missed It!
The Holy Scriptures................................18

Chapter 2: A Matter of Perspective
The Trinity................................24

Chapter 3: How Having a Father Helps Being a Father
The Father................................30

Chapter 4: The Courage to Be Nontraditional
The Son................................34

Chapter 5: Does God Have a Feminine Side?
The Holy Spirit................................38

Chapter 6: Creative Creatures
Creation................................44

Chapter 7: Free!
The Nature of Man................................50

Chapter 8: A Look Behind the Scenes
The Great Controversy................................56

Chapter 9: He Knows How Much I Can Take
The Life, Death, and Resurrection of Christ...........60

Chapter 10: Having Regrets Without Feeling Guilty
The Experience of Salvation................................66

Chapter 11: Thank God: Its Future Does Not Depend on Me
The Church................................70

Chapter 12: A Remnant of 50 Million?
The Remnant and Its Mission................................74

Chapter 13: Do You Want a McDonald's Church?
Unity in the Body of Christ................................80

Chapter 14: **Promises Are for Real**
Baptism 86

Chapter 15: **The Challenge of Servant-Leadership**
The Lord's Supper 90

Chapter 16: **Inspiration**
Spiritual Gifts and Ministries 94

Chapter 17: **Ellen G. White and My Denominational Career**
The Gift of Prophecy...100

Chapter 18: **No Sailing Under False Colors**
The Law of God...106

Chapter 19: **The Real Thing**
The Sabbath 112

Chapter 20: **First Things First**
Stewardship 118

Chapter 21: **Living XL**
Christian Behavior..124

Chapter 22: **"How is Mrs. Bruinsma?
How are the Children?"**
Marriage and the Family.....................................130

Chapter 23: **Bending Over Backward to Save Me!**
Christ's Ministry in the Heavenly Sanctuary.........136

Chapter 24: **Trusting in the One Who Is Coming**
The Second Coming of Christ 140

Chapter 25: **Safe (Saved) in God's Mercy**
Death and Resurrection 146

Chapter 26: **A Call to Mission**
The Millennium and the End of Sin 150

Chapter 27: **When Life Cannot Be Better**
The New Earth...154

The Truth Will Set Us Free

It happened some fifteen years ago, but I remember it like yesterday. I received a telephone call quite early in the morning. Could I immediately come to Amsterdam and visit a church member who was on the verge of death. He wanted to talk to me before he died. I was puzzled. I was not his pastor but worked at the time as the manager of the Adventist publishing house in the Netherlands. Why in the world would this man want to see me? Somehow I had a gut feeling that something was wrong. I phoned the local pastor, asked him to meet me, and agreed that we would go together.

Arriving at the home of our brother, we were told that he wanted to see only me. The local pastor remained in the living room with some family members and relatives while I went upstairs to the bedroom of our brother. He was obviously very weak but succeeded in instructing me to look under the bed, take the small tin box that was there, and open it. I did. To my great surprise it contained a large amount of money (about $20,000 I discovered later, when I had the opportunity to count it). He told me not to tell anyone of his family about this. "Take it," he said, "and use it for your work." I felt extremely uncomfortable but tried to give the visit a pastoral tone, prayed with him, and promised at his insistence that I would lead out at his funeral.

Returning to the living room, I was received with almost open hostility. An adult son asked me what his father had given me. I answered that I could not tell him. He phoned me later in the day and demanded to know whether I had received money from his father. If so, I must know that the money was not "kosher." I was in a predicament, for I had promised not to tell anyone about what had passed between his father and me, and yet I feared that the son might be right in suggesting that there was a story to the money that I ought to know. I told him not to worry about the money. His father was about to die. I would not touch the money for some time. If, after his father's death, I felt there was a need to investigate the matter further, I would contact him.

Our brother lived for another week. Long enough to receive a few more visits from his own pastor, during which he confessed where the money had come from. His sister had recently died. He had been entrusted with the task of looking after her estate. There was this amount in cash that she wanted to give to the Roman Catholic Church. And, being a true Seventh-day Adventist, this was just too much for him. To give so much money to the Catholics! It could be put to so much better use! He had decided to improve upon his sister's last wish and to channel it to where he felt it ought to go.

On a cold, rainy Friday afternoon I conducted the funeral service for our brother. The following Monday, I saw to it that the money reached its proper destination!

Even after so many years, this experience still haunts me. This brother was as "orthodox" in his beliefs as one could possibly be. Had he been alive today, he probably would have looked for at least a major portion of his spiritual food in publications from very conservative Adventist journals. I had been in his Sabbath School class a few times, and this had left me in no doubt that he was a staunch defender of all Adventist doctrines! But yet, on the brink of death, his religion did not prevent him from cheating on his sister posthumously and from stealing her money! How can something like this be explained? How is it possible that many decades of Christianity, of Bible reading, of study of the writings of Ellen White, of faithful church attendance and active participation in church programs can do so little to really change someone into a pleasant, outgoing, Christlike person? I know I must not judge our brother, but I cannot help wondering: How much does it really matter to give allegiance to all Adventist doctrines if it does not change us into real Christians?

I have used this experience quite a few times in worship talks or sermons to illustrate the dangerous gap that often exists between "orthodoxy" (believing the right thing) and "orthopraxis" (doing the right thing). I used it in a sermon I prepared some two or three years ago. This particular sermon was based on John 8:32: "Then you will know the truth, and the truth will set you free." What I tried to say was, in summary: It is not enough to have the truth as a theory, merely as a set of propositions, but the truth must do something for us. It must make a difference in our lives. Christ promises us that something will happen to us; having the truth will go beyond theoretical knowledge and will result in experience. The crucial question is: Do we become better, more balanced, more open, more pleasant, more Christian(!) people as a result of "having" the truth? Then I asked whether that question should not also be applied to our traditional Adventist understanding of truth: to the fundamental beliefs that we hold as a church. What do these fundamental beliefs really do for us? How do they change us? How do they make us happier, more balanced, more content, more trusting, more charitable, more open to others and their needs? In short: how do they make us better Christians? Because that must be the litmus test: Our doctrines must in some way not only remain external, theoretical propositions but must be translated into an internal, experiential truth that makes a difference in our lives. Then I proceeded in this sermon to illustrate what I meant by singling out three of our twenty-seven fundamental beliefs and by showing how these three doctrines may have a very concrete impact on our everyday existence. I finally challenged my audience to take the time to go through the full list of the twenty-seven doctrines, one by one, and to ask in each case: What does this doctrine mean for my life? How does it apply? How does it do something for me?

Well, we all know that preachers do not always practice what they preach. While I was exhorting my audience to look at each doctrine in this way, I vaguely realized that for many this might be a tall order. And also, that I should really go through this process myself before recommending it to others.

This book owes its origin to a large extent to the experience I had with my "orthodox" brother in Amsterdam, who so sadly failed in the domain of "orthopraxis," just days before his death, and to my sermon on John 8:32, which ended with the challenge I could not ignore myself. I realized it was time for me to take a good look at our church's beliefs and to see just how practical they really are.

Why have fundamental beliefs?

We should begin our look at our beliefs by asking some basic questions. Why does the Seventh-day Adventist Church have this impressive list of twenty-seven "fundamental beliefs"? Where do they come from? Was the list of doctrines compiled by a few prominent early Adventist leaders? Did Ellen White have a hand in it?

These are reasonable questions that deserve an answer before I take you on a personal tour of all these twenty-seven "fundamentals." As so often, we must begin with a bit of history.

Our current statement of fundamental beliefs dates from as recently as 1980. It replaced an earlier summary of Adventist doctrines that first appeared in 1931, which in turn replaced the "Declaration of the Fundamental Principles Taught and Practiced by the Seventh-day Adventists" of 1872.

Admittedly, 1872 is a long time ago. Nonetheless, this was the first official declaration, which means that it was almost three decades after Adventism had begun to develop from its Millerite roots before any official doctrinal statement was formulated. The first generation of Adventist leaders had a thorough dislike for anything that looked or sounded like an official creed or confessional statement. This was partly the result of their experience: In the final phase of the Millerite Movement many had been disfellowshiped by traditional churches that proudly championed the historic creeds and confessions of faith but nonetheless rejected truth when it was presented to them. Their bitter experience in October 1844, when their expectations failed to materialize, no doubt also contributed to their reluctance to spell out their beliefs in great detail in any kind of official way. And it must be remembered that a number of the most important leaders of this early period, such as Joseph Bates and James White, had been members of the Christian Connection, a Christian group of mostly Methodist background that greatly objected to formal creeds. This denomination had taken the position that the Bible would be its only creed and that a Christian character would be its only test of fellowship.

Against that background we understand his paucity of words when James White, in 1845, responded to the question what Adventists believe with these words: "The Bible is a perfect, and complete revelation. It is our only rule of faith and practice" (*A Word to the Little Flock,* 13). Two years later Present Truth, the earliest Seventh-day Adventist periodical, contained a similar statement: "The Bible is our chart—our guide. It is our only rule of faith and practice, to which we would closely adhere" (Dec. 1849, 46).

However, as time went by and the church began to grow, a clear need was felt to have a "synopsis of our faith." And so, reluctantly, in 1872 a summary of Adventist beliefs was published. The introductory paragraph of this statement that consisted of twenty-five "articles" is worth quoting at some length:

> In presenting to the public this synopsis of our faith, we wish it to be distinctly understood that we have no articles of faith, creed, or discipline, aside from the Bible. We do not put forth this as having any authority with our people, nor is it designed to secure uniformity among them, as a system of faith, but it is a brief statement of what is, and has been, with great unanimity, held by them. We often find it necessary to meet enquiries on this subject, and sometimes to correct false statements circulated against us, and to remove erroneous impressions which have obtained with those who have not had opportunity to become acquainted with our faith and practice. . . . The following propositions . . . aim to be a concise statement of the more prominent features of our faith.

The statement of beliefs of 1872 is very interesting in what it mentions but not less so in what it fails to mention. One of its most striking features is the omission of any reference to a belief in the Trinity. Those who know something about Adventist history realize that this basic Christian teaching was at that time not yet fully accepted by the Adventist believers. And there are other indications in this document that Adventist theology was still in a process of development.

The 1931 statement of "Fundamental Beliefs" that served the church for almost fifty years was much closer to our current statement than to the earlier one of 1872. It was intended to summarize "the principal features" of "certain fundamental beliefs" (twenty-two in all), "together with a portion of the Scriptural references upon which they are based." The 1931 statement was formulated by four "leading brethren" without any input from others. When, in the seventies, the church felt the need to take another good look at its statement of beliefs, a much more thorough and more careful process was devised, which led to the acceptance of our current statement of the twenty-seven fundamental beliefs by the delegates at the General Conference session of 1980 in Dallas, Texas.

Again I would like to quote the introductory paragraph. Regrettably this is often omitted when the statement is printed in full (even in the Seventh-day Adventist Yearbook!) Yet these words are vital for a correct appreciation of the value and limitations of this important document:

> Seventh-day Adventists accept the Bible as their only creed and hold certain fundamental beliefs to be the teachings of the Holy Scriptures. These beliefs, as set forth here, constitute the church's understanding and expression of the teaching of Scripture. Revision of these statements may be expected at a General Conference session when the church is led by the Holy Spirit to a fuller understanding of Bible truths or finds better language in which to express the teachings of God's Holy Word.

Well, that briefly answers the question of how we arrived at our current statement of fundamental beliefs. It is the result of a long development. Of course, it is now much more difficult to modify a statement of beliefs than it was a century or even half a century ago. Our church is not immune to the tendency to cultivate traditions. Moreover, the church has become so big and so complex that the process of changing even a few words would be a very complicated and time-consuming one. But although the statement will probably be with us for quite some time, let us not forget that we have never wanted a statement that is set in concrete forever. We have resisted the type of creedal formulas that are routinely recited in archaic language but hardly understood. We have resisted the arrogant pretense that we would be able to perfectly summarize and phrase the essence of the teachings of the Bible, with no need for any change, improvement, or adaptation ever. We have admitted that we need to always continue in our search for a deeper meaning of biblical truth and must have the humility to discard views that, after all, do not hold up in the light of divine revelation or may be misunderstood as the world around us changes. Therefore, when I take you on this pilgrimage along the twenty-seven "fundamentals," it is with this preamble in mind that these statements are neither perfect nor final. They may be remodified again as times goes by. But this statement summarizes as best as the corporate church can say it at this time what we as Adventists believe.

But before we embark on our trip, I would like to add just a few further remarks. Is it really necessary to have such a set of doctrines? Has history not taught us that doctrinal discussions often generate more heat than light? Can one not simply believe in the Bible, in God, and in Jesus and what He has done for us? If doctrines are so important, how do we explain that we do not find a list of basic doctrines in the Bible?

Actually, this last claim is not totally true, for there are some very significant doctrinal statements in the New Testament. We find some profound theological (or doctrinal, if you prefer that term) pronouncements like: "Jesus is Lord" (Romans 10:9-12), and: "I [Christ] and the Father are one" (John 10:30). A fairly elaborate statement appears in 1 Timothy 3:16, where it is said of Jesus Christ that "He was revealed in the flesh, vindicated in the Spirit, seen by angels, proclaimed among the Gentiles, believed in throughout the world, taken up in glory." And toward the end of the first letter of

Paul to the Corinthians (15:1-8) we find an even fuller "statement of beliefs":

> Now, brothers, I want to remind you of the gospel I preached to you, which you have received and on which you have taken your stand. By this gospel you are saved, if you hold firmly to the word I preached to you. Otherwise you have believed in vain. For what I have received I passed on to you as of first importance: that Christ died for our sins according to the Scriptures, that He was buried, that He was raised on the third day according to the Scriptures, and that He appeared to Peter, and then to the Twelve. After that He appeared to more than five hundred at the same time, most of whom are still living, though some have fallen asleep. Then He appeared to James, then to all the apostles, and last of all He appeared to me also, as to one abnormally born.

We notice the repeated warning against false teachings and teachers (2 Peter 2:1; 2 Timothy 4:3; 1 Timothy 1:10; Ephesians. 4:14) and exhortations to follow sound scriptural teachings (Titus 2:7; 1 Tim. 4:16) and to "correctly handle the word of truth" (2 Timothy 2:15). These texts illustrate that the apostles considered correct doctrine to be important. Thus, when doctrinal disagreements threatened to undermine the unity of the church, a church council was convened to solve the problems (Acts 15).

Doctrinal statements are unavoidable. We say that we believe in God. And that we want to follow Jesus Christ. These simple affirmations raise all sorts of questions. Who and what is the God we believe in? What did He do for us, what is He currently doing for us, and what will He do for us in the future? How does He differ from us human beings? Why is it important that we believe in Jesus Christ? He lived and died, but what makes his life and death meaningful for me? What can it possibly mean when we talk about a Trinity of Father, Son, and Holy Spirit? And what does it mean when the Bible tells us that Christ ascended into heaven and will come again? What implications does it have when we say that God is our Creator? What do we refer to when we call the Bible inspired? What exactly is sin? And how do we deal with it? The list of questions could go on.

We cannot just say that we believe, without asking questions and looking for answers. We need to know what our faith implies. What demands it makes on us. What blessings it has in store for us. Doctrines help us to order the basic information about the Bible, about God, and salvation. They are a means to chart our beliefs and a compass to help us stay out of the shallow waters of heresy. Doctrines and statements of belief are not more important than the Bible. Rather, they help us to systematize the biblical teachings in human categories. Doctrines are couched in human, and therefore imperfect, terms. They always reflect the times in which they were formulated—in what they say and in what they omit, and certainly in the emphases they place on certain aspects of the Christian faith. Statements of belief are, therefore, never the final word. As finite human beings we will never get "to the bottom" of things when we are searching the infinite riches of the divine revelation. But without doctrines our faith loses structure and might easily wander in the wrong direction. Our thinking needs the guidance of the corporate thinking of our fellow-believers of past and present. Truth is not to be equated with doctrines. Truth surpasses any set of doctrines, but doctrinal statements provide a safe framework for our quest for truth.

Authors do not always write all chapters of a book in the order in which they finally appear in print. In writing this book, I completed most of the chapters before writing this introduction. I can assure you that this book has been more difficult to write than anything I have ever produced before. But it has been a tremendous personal blessing to complete the task that I had set myself: to extract some deep personal meaning from each of the twenty-seven fundamental beliefs. I hope it will encourage many readers to embark on a similar exploration.

"Having" the right doctrines is important, but doctrinal truth means nothing if it is only intellectual assent and does not impact on us in a very personal way; if it does not change us; if it does not "set us free." There is no doubt that God is more interested in what we do with our faith than how we talk about it or write about it. Around 450 B.C. the prophet Malachi complained that the religion of the people of God was empty ritual and nothing else. "Oh, that one of you would shut the temple doors, so that you would not light useless fires on my altar! I am not pleased with you, says the Lord Almighty" (Malachi 1:10). Reading the four brief chapters of the book of Malachi we are left in no doubt: God is weary of all the things his people say and all the empty acts of worship they perform. Their religious activity is meaningless as long as it remains a matter of pious propositions and holy customs, rather than a force that changes them and affects them in a personal way. Christ echoed exactly the same sentiments when He told His audience that the ultimate question is not whether we can pass an exam in systematic theology but whether our lives have been touched by His contagious love (Matthew 25:31-46).

Years ago I read a story about Don Pedro, a priest in Mexico, who boarded up the doors of his church. He put a sign on the front porch: Closed until further notice. Why had Don Pedro decided to take such drastic measures? For several weeks he had tried everything he could to find accommodations for a homeless couple but to no avail. None of his parishioners volunteered to take these poor people in. Don Pedro felt that church services were a total waste of effort as long as his people showed no desire to put at least some of the basics of Christianity into practice. His radical methodology worked. In no time the homeless couple had a roof over their head.

Don Pedro was on the right track: if the Christian religion does not do something for us and make us "authentic Christians" in the way we think and act, we might as well close the church. Rather than closing my church, however, I would like to see it become more and more a community where the truth is not only proclaimed and discussed but first of all experienced and lived!

1 The Holy Scriptures

The Holy Scriptures, Old and New Testaments, are the written Word of God, given by divine inspiration through holy men of God who spoke and wrote as they were moved by the Holy Spirit. In this Word, God has committed to man the knowledge necessary for salvation. The Holy Scriptures are the infallible revelation of His will. They are the standard of character, the test of experience, the authoritative revealer of doctrines, and the trustworthy record of God's acts in history.

2 Peter 1:20, 21;

2 Tim. 3:16, 17;

Ps. 119:105;

Prov. 30:5, 6;

Isa. 8:20;

John 17:17;

1 Thess. 2:13;

Heb. 4:12.

Chapter 1

"How to read the Bible" is a hot topic in the Adventist Church. Some Adventists believe that every word of Scripture is verbally inspired. But that is not official church teaching. As Adventists we have gone on record that we believe that the writers and not the words of the Bible were inspired. Thus, although we take a very "high" view of Scripture, we have rejected verbal inspiration and allow for the human element in the Bible. But just how small or how large is this human aspect? That question will keep Adventist theologians busy for quite a few more years, I suppose.

I must admit that I follow the debate with keen interest but not because I hope that this will finally help me to sort out this problem for myself. Some two decades ago this topic was high on my list of things that needed to be clarified. At one time I worried greatly about some discrepancies and historical inaccuracies in the Bible that I felt could not be overlooked. I read extensively about this issue, making sure to get different perspectives. I remember how helpful a little book by Gerhard Bergmann was. This German book (with the title *Alarm um die Bibel—Alarm Concerning the Bible*), very succinctly describes the problem, masterfully defends the absolute authority of the Bible, while giving full due to the divine and the human element in the writing down of God's Word, and relativizing the few so-called internal contradictions and inaccuracies. I have always remembered Bergmann's counsel: With regard to these elements in Scripture that trouble us, we should assume the attitude of "ein frohliches Unbekumertsein" (a happy absence of worry). That has been my attitude deep down ever since.

I am, of course, aware of another issue concerning the Bible that looms large in current Adventist debates: the question of how we are to read the Bible. There used to be, and unfortunately still is, quite a bit of irresponsible prooftext methodology around. Texts are skillfully combined in a particular order to prove a point, without much attention for the context in which these texts are found. Adventists are slowly moving away from this and paying closer attention to the context. But other concerns remain. How is the text to be understood? What is literal? What is symbolic? How do we discover the unchanging principle under the layer of cultural expression? Why is it that we agree that Bible texts about slavery must be understood within the framework of the time and culture in which they were written, while many remain adamant that some texts about the role of women must be taken literally? I feel quite frustrated when I see this confusion, and I fervently hope that our church will make progress in formulating a clearer hermeneutic (that is the technical term for the methodology of interpreting the Bible). Too many of our members are still clinging to a form of fundamentalism that arbitrarily chooses to interpret certain statements as either literal or symbolic, based more on what they wish to believe than on sound Bible study.

But my main problem with the Bible is at a different level. I have always found it difficult to come to terms with the many "gory" stories of the Old Testament. This struck me again very vividly some time ago, when we studied the book of Judges in the Sabbath School. One of our lessons zeroed in on the story of Ehud who assassinated Eglon, the fat Moabite king. The story is told in graphic detail, as are many of the other stories in the same Bible book and in other historical sections of the Bible. When I read these stories, I cannot help but wonder: Is this God's inspired Word? How do these stories help me to become more spiritual? They tend to turn me off and diminish my zeal for Bible reading instead of strengthening it. I know I should try to extract some lessons even from those ancient tales of violence and destruction, but that does not come easy.

But just as there are moments when I almost despair of what I read, there are moments when I realize: Yes, this is God's Word for me. This so directly touches me, that I sense in a way I cannot express in words, that indeed the Bible is the divinely inspired guide that keeps me on the straight and narrow. Just the other day I was reading in the Psalms, using the paraphrase by the Presbyterian poet and theology professor Eugene H. Peterson. The words of Psalm 73 were so powerful and were so true for me. They "hit" me as never before:

No doubt about it! God is good—
good to good people, good to the good-hearted.
But I nearly missed it,
missed seeing his goodness.
I was looking the other way,
looking up to the people
At the top,
envying the wicked who have it made,
Who have nothing to worry about
not a care in the whole wide world . . .

Still, when I tried to figure it out
all I got was a splitting headache . . .
Until I entered the sanctuary of God.

Then I saw the whole picture . . .
I'm in the very presence of God—
oh, how refreshing it is!
I've made the Lord God my home.
God, I'm telling the world what you do!

I know one has to be careful with paraphrases. But we need translations and paraphrases that communicate the Word to us in the language of our time. As someone for whom English is a second language, I feel uncomfortable with the King James Version, and even with the RSV. I have grown rather fond of the New International Version, but people like Eugene Peterson have helped me a great deal to better appreciate some of the beautiful and utterly relevant promises of the Psalms. I cannot resist quoting one more passage from his paraphrase:

Don't put your life in the hands of experts
who know nothing of life, of salvation life.
Mere humans don't have what it takes;
when they die, their projects die with them.
Instead, get help from the God of Jacob,
put your hope in God and know real blessing! (146: 3, 4).

When I hear God's Word so loud and clear, I truly am *frohlich unbekummert* about many of the technical details in the theological debate about inspiration and hermeneutics. After all, hearing the Word is so much more important than hearing arguments—words about the Word!

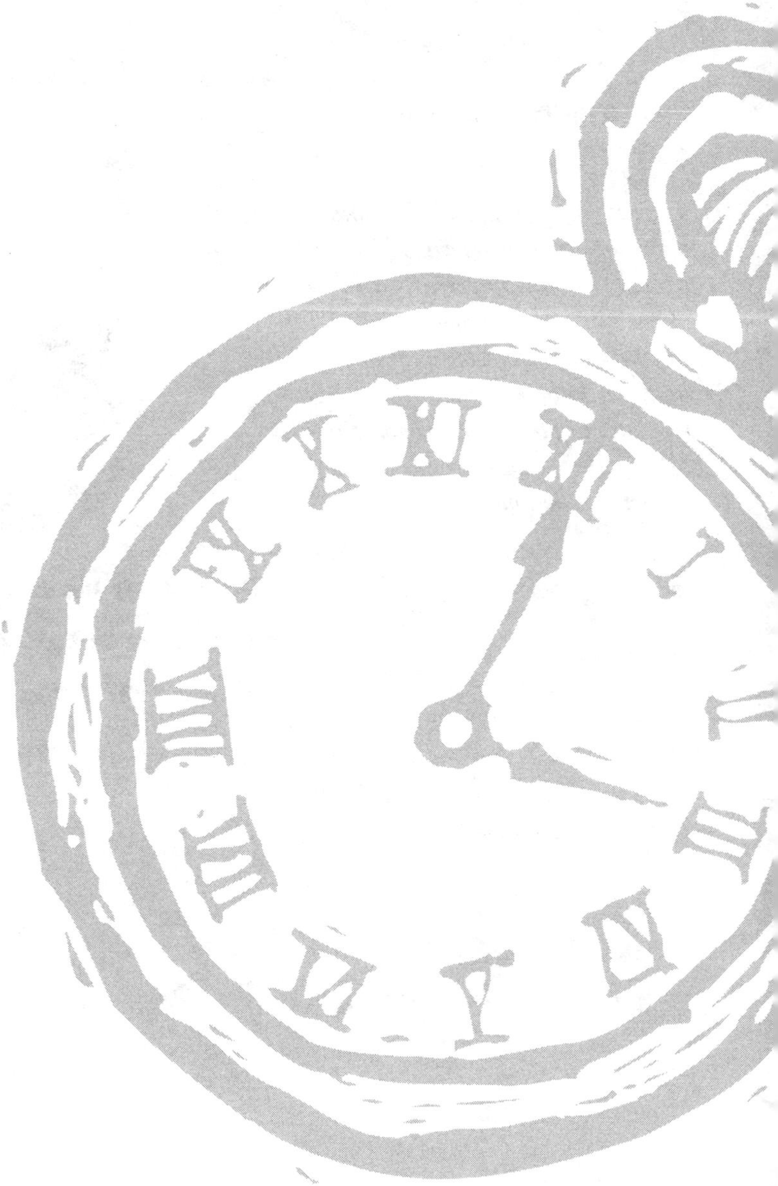

2 | The Trinity

There is one God: Father, Son, and Holy Spirit, a unity of three co-eternal Persons. God is immortal, all-powerful, all-knowing, above all, and ever present. He is infinite and beyond human comprehension, yet known through His self-revelation. He is forever worthy of worship, adoration, and service by the whole creation.

Deut. 6:4; Matt. 28:19;

2 Cor. 13:14; Eph. 4:4-6;

1 Peter 1:2; 1 Tim. 1:17;

Rev. 14:7.

Chapter 2

A Matter of Perspective

During my graduate study in theology, I had to read a few hundred pages from one of the volumes of Karl Barth's *Christian Dogmatics*. This German theologian has written the kind of books that require about an hour per page if you want to get some idea of what he is trying to say. The chapters I had to read were related to the Godhead and dealt in particular with the concept of the Trinity. Though it was heavy going at the time, I am still glad that I had to read this. Had it not been compulsory, I probably would never have had the courage to wrestle with all those involved sentences and all the fine print in the footnotes. These many hours of hard work have, however, made a significant impact on my thinking about God. I was forced to wrestle with the paradox that Christians believe in one God, while in the same breath they affirm that there are three Persons: Father, Son, and Holy Spirit. How in the world can that be: one, and yet three? Karl Barth told me: Do not try to understand this, for you never will. You must accept that God is one. As soon as you are willing to entertain the possibility that there is more than one God, you have ceased to be a Christian, and you have become a pagan polytheist (a worshiper of more than one god). But if you do not recognize that somehow there are three "persons"—Father, Son, and Holy Spirit—who are on the same

25

level and are distinct from each other—you likewise have lost the Christian concept of God.

Try as you may, you will never be able to arrive at a formula that will do justice to the element of one-ness and that of three-ness in the Godhead. If you overemphasize the one-ness, you automatically do injustice to the three-ness, and you virtually say that there are not three persons but that God sometimes puts on the "mask" of the Father, while at other times He wears that of the Son or of the Holy Spirit. If, on the other hand, you overemphasize the three-ness you end up with a heavenly Board of Directors rather than with the one God of the Bible. Studying this complicated subject brought home to me as never before that human beings can never hope to define God. We simply do not have what it takes to even come close to understanding who and what God is. We employ terms that enable us to discuss the topic, but as soon as we have made our doctrinal statements about God, we must reverently step back and say: What we have just stated does not in any way do justice to Him. He is infinitely greater than anything we can say!

What can I know?

This does not apply only when we deal with the one-ness and three-ness of God but also when we use words such as eternal, almighty, omniscient, and omnipresent.

What do I know about being eternal, about being without beginning and without end? I know about my beginning, and that is nothing to brag about. I was born in a rather poor neighborhood in Amsterdam just before the end of the Second World War, grew up in small village that very few people have ever heard of, in a very simple home. And although I do not know when my life will end, I know it will one day. I realize that I must count the remainder of my life not in terms of centuries, but in years, or at most in decades. So what do I know of eternity?

What do I know about being almighty? I may have a bit of authority in the church, but what does that really mean? When, as a division representative, I travel to areas in the territory of the division I serve, I will usually get a friendly reception and will be politely listened to, but if anything is going to stick of what I say, it is not because of any status I may have in the church but because I happen to say something that makes sense or otherwise strikes a chord. My authority, if I have any, is very limited. Even my wife does not always do what I suggest (nor should she). And there are lots of things in my life I cannot change. So what do I know about being almighty?

What do I know about being omniscient? I am fortunate in that I have a university education and lead the kind of life that constantly teaches me new things. I am an avid reader and am blessed with an inquisitive mind. Although I have not pursued an academic career, I keep up reasonably well with publications in my discipline. But there are so many things I know nothing about. I divide birds into two categories: flying birds and floating birds. That is about all I know about that part of the animal kingdom. My wife is always keen on going to an arboretum or a botanical garden. Somehow she knows the names of hundreds of species, while I have difficulty distinguishing an oak from a birch tree. I know nothing about physics, have forgotten the most simple algebraic formulas, and am totally ignorant when it come to cricket, gardening, and setting a VCR—just to mention a few examples of a list that could be extended ad infinitum. So, what do I know about omniscience?

What do I know about being omnipresent? Sure, it helps to have a telephone, and one of these days I am going to buy myself a mobile phone. Carrying my laptop computer wherever I go and checking my e-mail several times a day does at times give me the illusion that I am still in the office while in fact I am hundreds or even thousands of miles away from it. Nonetheless, the truth is that I can still only be at one place at any one time. So, what do I know about omnipresence?

God and me

Thinking about God, I get a much better perspective on myself. Like most people, I easily fall into the temptation of comparing myself with other people. And, again like most people, I have the tendency to be selective in doing so. I make sure that the comparison works in my favor. I like to think of myself as a bit smarter, a bit more sophisticated, a bit more influential than most people. But even if my perception is right, this does not give me grounds for considering myself a notch or two elevated above other people.

For two reasons. First, if I compare myself with others and my abilities with theirs, I must be honest enough also to look at those whose IQ is much higher than mine and those who are superior to me in a zillion different ways!

Second, any such comparison is rather irrelevant. I have a few basic attributes in common with other people that are far more important than the things that make me different from them. I am mortal, just like anyone else. I am just as powerless as anyone else when it comes to changing my gender, the color of my skin, or my hair. Just like everyone else, I did not have free choice in selecting my parents, nor do I control most of the factors that could either lengthen or shorten my life. I am utterly limited in what I can do and experience. Just like all other human beings, past, present, and future, I am a finite creature before an infinite Creator.

Ever since reading Barth on the topic of the Trinity, I have come back to this fundamental truth: I am a creature with all that the term implies. God is the Creator. He is in a totally different category—all by Himself. I grope for words when I try to describe Him: Trinity, almighty, omnipresent, or whatever terms I use, I never fully get a handle on who and what God is. Over the years I have increasingly realized how futile it is to think that it will ever be otherwise. And praise God for that. There are plenty of beings like me, either just like me or slightly less intelligent, powerful, sophisticated, etc. than I, or slightly more so. I appreciate what they can do for me when I am in a bind, but usually their assistance is pretty limited. There is One who is not like our fellow creatures, because He is the Creator. His involvement in my life can make a real difference, for He is infinitely greater. Most people may not need to read heavy books on theology before they truly understand this, but in my case it was a great help, for which I continue to be grateful.

3 The Father

*God the Eternal Father is the Creator, Source,
Sustainer, and Sovereign of all creation. He
is just and holy, merciful and gracious,
slow to anger, and abounding in
steadfast love and faithfulness. The
qualities and powers exhibited in
the Son and the Holy Spirit are
also revelations of the Father.*

Gen. 1:1; Rev. 4:11;

1 Cor. 15:28; John 3:16;

1 John 4:8; 1 Tim. 1:17;

Exod. 34:6, 7; John 14:9.

Chapter 3

How Having a Father Helps Being a Father

To say that God is our Father bothers some people nowadays. They believe that speaking of God in masculine terms perpetuates injustice toward women, for it highlights the bias of men who continue to live with outdated concepts from patriarchal times. These people insist that we must abandon such terms in favor of gender-inclusive language, addressing God as our heavenly Parent. Some would go so far as to insist that we must try to compensate for centuries of one-sidedness by speaking of the Divine as our heavenly Mother.

To many of us this kind of approach smacks too much of a liberal radicalism. The Bible calls God "our Father," and who are we that we should try to correct this inspired analogy?

I must admit that I still feel a little uneasy when I hear God addressed as "Mother" or even as our "heavenly Parent." Yet, I know that even in the Bible such notions are not totally absent. In several instances the image of motherhood is used in connection with God (see, for example, Matthew 23:37; Luke 13:34). No, there is no biblical or theological problem with also using female categories when we try to define the indefinable.

Beyond definition

It is important that we realize that we can never define God in human words. The best we can do is use analogies.

We must keep that in mind when we call God a "person." What we want to say is that God relates to us in a personal way. But his "personhood" includes much more than ours. Nonetheless, the word does help us to say something meaningful about God. The same is true when we call God "our Father." God is not a father (or a mother or a parent, for that matter) in the ordinary sense of the word. Yet, the word says something very profound about God. It says something about His relationship to us, about His authority over us, and about His love and constant care for us.

How does thinking about God as a Father affect me personally? Very profoundly. Fatherhood is an important aspect of my life. My father died after a prolonged illness when I was only fourteen. I must be careful not to judge him. His was not an easy life, and the knowledge that his physical condition would continue to deteriorate, would leave him an invalid and bring him to an early grave, must have been a terrible burden. But, sadly enough, I don't remember him as a very caring father. And looking back at my teens and adolescence, I now begin to understand how not having a father in those years left a void that was never really filled. I have come to realize how important it is to have a father who is there for you, someone whose strength you can rely on, someone you can count on—someone who will be understanding and forgiving when you do things your own way but will continue to stimulate you in making the right choices.

Now, years later, I see other aspects of fatherhood. I have now been a father for many years. Being a partner is an extremely fulfilling experience, but so is being a father. My experience as a father helps me to more fully appreciate the image of God as a Father. But it also helps me to see the infinite difference between me as a human father and my heavenly Father. Just think for a minute about how God our Father is described in fundamental belief number three. Apart from being the Creator, the Source, the Sustainer, and Sovereign of all creation, He is also said to be "just and holy, merciful and gracious, slow to anger, and abounding in steadfast love and faithfulness."

I try, in my own limited way, to show love and faithfulness. I trust that those who are close to me, in particular my wife and (adult) children, have recognized through the years, and still sense, love and faithfulness. But I know I have fallen short in many ways, when it comes to being just and holy. At times I think I have shown myself to be quite merciful, but I realize that often I have been less than gracious, and I could certainly not claim that I am slow to anger. Unfortunately, I must admit that I am a rather miserable father, when I compare my fatherhood with God's fatherhood.

Seeing both sides

So the image of God as my Father works in two directions. First, it helps me get another glimpse of what God is. He is the ideal father. The kind of father I never had and the kind of father I will never be. He is more firmly attached to me and is more deeply interested in me and committed to my total well-being (again using very human terms) than I will ever be in my relationship with my children. And, of course, that is good to know. It is a liberating thought that the Sovereign God is not primarily the Ruler and the Judge, but He is first of all the loving Father. And, second, thinking about God as the Father spurs me to want to be—better late than never—a better father myself.

Please feel free to substitute words like Mother and Parent in the previous paragraphs. But, being a male, I cannot help but continue to be greatly stimulated by the idea of having a heavenly Father.

4 The Son

God the eternal Son became incarnate in Jesus
Christ. Through Him all things were created, the character of God is revealed,
the salvation of humanity is accomplished, and the world is judged.
Forever truly God, He became also
truly man, Jesus the Christ. He
was conceived of the Holy
Spirit and born of the virgin
Mary. He lived and experienced temptation as a
human being, but perfectly
exemplified the righteousness
and the love of God. By His
miracles He manifested
God's power and was attested
as God's promised Messiah.
He suffered and died volun-
tarily on the cross for our sins
and in our place, was raised
from the dead, and ascended to
minister in the heavenly sanctuary
in our behalf. He will come again in
glory for the final deliverance of His people and the restoration of all things.

John 1:1-3, 14;

Col. 1:15-19; John 10:30;

14:9; Rom. 6:23;

2 Cor. 5:17-19; John 5:22;

Luke 1:35; Phil. 2:5-11;

Heb. 2:9-18; 1 Cor. 15:3, 4;

Heb. 8:1, 2; John 14:1-3.

Chapter 4

The Courage to Be Nontraditional

I will not quarrel with you if you say that Harry Anderson was a great artist. And I will not argue if you insist that his work has been a blessing to many people. But I cannot stand his pictures of Jesus. To me they portray Jesus as a sweet but unreal, out-of-this-world, character whom I have difficulty relating to.

When, in the eighties, I worked in Africa, I often saw Jesus depicted as black. At first that worried me somewhat. Was it permissible for African believers to draw Jesus into their own world? After all, to make Jesus a Black seems an injustice to history. But then I realized it is just as much historically incorrect to depict Jesus as a European, an Indian, or an American as it is to picture Him as an African. If we want to paint or sculpt Him as He really was, we must rather look for our model in the Middle East.

I believe that Jesus became man in a universal sense. He became one of us. He became a Jew some two thousand years ago. But in a very profound sense He also became an Indian, a Yoruba, a Korean, an American, and a Dutchman. In some profound way His manhood represents every form and shade of manhood that ever existed and ever will exist on this earth. It is important for me to grasp that fact, because only if I can see Him as a Dutchman of the late 20th century, can He really become my brother and can I really regard Him as my role model.

Role model

We all need role models. In retrospect I blame much of my erratic behavior in my early teens on the fact that I had no father and had few if any role models. But, fortunately, as I grew older, there were such role models who helped me to develop my personality and to pursue realistic goals in a more consistent way. I hope that I in turn, at least to some degree, have become a role model for others—in particular, for my children.

I know there are many aspects of Christ's life that demand our attention. I try to understand what it means that He has come to deal with my sins, that He has died for me. We will return to that topic elsewhere in this book. I believe that His coming to this earth was miraculous: He was born of a virgin. I have decided not to worry too much about the "mechanics" of a virgin birth; I am content with the thought that it stands to reason that when something so exceptional happens—when God becomes a man; when divinity takes on humanity—we may well expect this to occur in a unique manner. I have spent quite some time thinking about miracles in general and Christ's miracles in particular. In fact, some years ago I wrote a book on this topic. I have wrestled in my mind with many of the issues involved, but my belief in miracles has been strengthened as a result of that exercise.

However, when I ponder what Jesus means for my everyday life, my mind does not turn to His miracles, but it keeps coming back to this concept of a role model. There are some traits in Jesus' character, some elements in the way He went about His work and interacted with people, that I find highly attractive and want to emulate. Let me single out one thing: He was nontraditional.

Breaking with tradition

Christ did what He believed in. He did not just do what was politically correct and what would further His career. It certainly was not politically correct to talk with the woman at the well, to eat in the house of a non-Jewish tax collector, or to chase the money-changers from the temple court. It did not enhance His career to choose Gallilean fishermen as His close associates and to make claims for Himself that were bound to be understood as blasphemy.

He did not do away with eternal principles but took the liberty to clothe these in more relevant forms. For example, He kept the Sabbath but refused to be hostage to traditional patterns of Sabbath observance that took all the joy out of the weekly day of rest and (very literally) re-creation.

Christ stood for what He believed. He rejected tradition for the sake of tradition. He was willing to take the risk that He would be misunderstood. He worked for change, uninhibitedly and consistently. He always looked beyond mere externals and went for the core of things. That took courage in the kind of society He was born into.

I would like to see some major changes in my church. So many of the things we do and so many of the ways in which we say things need to be changed. Although the basic truths of the Adventist version of the Christian faith are nonnegotiable, we must find ways to make our beliefs more relevant. Our church must be a workshop and not a museum. But it is seldom wise to rock the boat! It is much easier to be remain silent, or to act and speak in a politically correct way. But we must be willing to take risks in speaking out against tradition and in favor of new ways of doing and saying things. I realize that I am not as consistent as He was, and that I make errors of judgment as I try to find new ways and words. But to me "following Jesus" means taking Him as my role model and being courageous enough to be nontraditional in the way I talk and live my faith, focused on the core of things rather than on externals that have become meaningless by the passing of time.

5 The Holy Spirit

God the eternal Spirit was active with the
Father and the Son in Creation, incarna-
tion, and redemption. He inspired the
writers of Scripture. He filled Christ's
life with power, He draws and con-
victs human beings; and those
who respond He renews and
transforms into the image of
God. Sent by the Father and
the Son to be always with His
children, He extends spiritual gifts to the church,
empowers it to bear witness
to Christ, and in harmony
with the Scriptures leads it
into all truth.

Gen. 1:1, 2; Luke 1:35; 4:18;

Acts 10:38; 2 Peter 1:21;

2 Cor. 3:18; Eph. 4:11, 12;

Acts 1:8; John 14:16-18, 26;

15:26, 27; 16:7-13.

Chapter 5

Does God Have a Feminine Side?

One thing you can be pretty sure of when you go to a Seventh-day Adventist church in Scandinavia, Germany, or Holland is that there will be no altar calls—unless there is a foreign speaker! I remember in my teens going to a youth congress where a General Conference dignitary was the main speaker. For the last twenty or so minutes of his sermon the audience was becoming increasingly uneasy. He was slowly but unmistakably moving toward the climax, and we somehow knew it: Before too long he would want us to get out of our seats, maybe raise our hands, or even worse, come forward! For me it spoiled most of the morning. Would I get up when the call would be made? Or would I dare to stay seated while others around me reluctantly would get to their feet?

This uneasiness toward altar calls and other forms of "emotional religion" are still firmly embedded in me. A number of years ago I was conducting an evangelistic campaign for students at the University of Antananarivo, in Madagascar. The meetings went quite well. I remained my natural self, rather rational in approach, and people seemed to respond positively. But after about ten programs the local pastors felt that it was about time for an altar call, and they conveyed that message to me as tactfully as they could.

The following evening I decided I would try it. No one was more surprised than I when several hundred people came forward! However, I am still reluctant when it comes to this type of thing.

Rational religion

This difficulty in relating to outward, emotional stimuli is partly cultural. Deep down there are some Dutch Reformed streaks in my Adventism, as there are some Lutheran streaks in my Scandinavian brethren! But it is more than local, cultural baggage. Adventists in general are in many ways very rational in what they believe. From the beginning of our movement there has been a fear of emotional fanaticism. Feelings should not take over, we believe, for they can easily lead us astray!

That type of thinking has influenced our attitude toward the Holy Spirit. We know He exists. We profess that He is important. We believe that He was working mightily when the church started in the apostolic age. And we understand from a number of prophetic statements that there will be a renewed "outpouring" of the Spirit before the second coming of Christ takes place. But we are very skeptical about manifestations of the Spirit in the present! We do not want the kind of thing that we see in Pentecostal circles. We are so scared of the type of phenomena that accompany the "Toronto blessing" and the emotional scenes at popular faith-healing services that we prefer to keep the Spirit at arm's length.

When you think about this a little further, this is indeed quite remarkable. We believe that God has given spiritual gifts to His church. We have zeroed in on the gift of prophecy and subsequently have totally identified the "spirit of prophecy" with the ministry of Ellen G. White. That is where, for all practical purposes in Adventism, the prophetic gift stopped, and we would be very reluctant to entertain the idea that it could be manifested in other persons in a similar way. We do not welcome any speaking in tongues, and we have by and large relegated the gift of healing to the scientific methods approved by our medical institutions.

In saying this about my church, I am in fact describing my own feelings. But lately I have more and more realized that the church ought to be more open to all the gifts of the Spirit. And as I have had the opportunity to travel in other parts of the world and observe how Adventism manifests itself elsewhere, I have also come to realize that this openness does in fact exist to a much larger degree in some non-Western environments. There are places in the world where exorcisms by Adventist pastors are routine and where the exercise of the gift of healing is quite common. And where people still expect God to speak to them through dreams!

What about the Spirit?

On the other hand, I also believe that the power of the Holy Spirit manifests itself not only, not even primarily, in the spectacular phenomena that occurred in apostolic times. Being "filled with the Spirit" does not necessarily demand that we shout hallelujah's when it is not part of our culture to do so; nor does responding to the promptings of the Spirit necessarily involve the outward physical action of moving to the front of the church after an altar call. The Spirit may in some instances come in flames of fire but will usually attract our attention by speaking with a "still small voice."

The Spirit is very real. He is more than an impersonal influence. He is God, the third Person of the Trinity. That is correct theology, but what does it tell me? Some biblical descriptions may actually be more helpful. God is present with us through His Spirit. The Spirit helps us to have a true picture of ourselves as sinners and convinces us of the need for conversion. He guides us, brings things to our mind. He comforts us. He tells us how to pray. He sanctifies us. Those terms do not suggest power in terms of physical force but rather as tender care and loving support. In that connection it is interesting to remember that in the early church the Spirit was at times referred to in feminine terms. We find examples in the literature of the early Jewish-Christian community and of the early church in Syria, as well as in the writing of some of the church fathers. Admittedly, not everything the early Christian writers have said is biblically correct. But this may be an insight that we should consider. We must realize that describing God as male or female is inadequate, but since we habitually use the pronoun "He" when we refer to God, we might at least occasionally also think in terms of "She" when we try to understand a little better what the Spirit does for us. (If this little exercise makes you too uncomfortable, simply substitute masculine pronouns for the feminine ones in the next two paragraphs.)

That She does something for me is undeniable. Even though I do not speak in tongues—and to be honest have no desire to do so. Even though I have not laid my hands on sick people during a healing service or cast out any demons. Yes, even though I am still reluctant in urging people to respond to the promptings of the Spirit by asking them to come forward, I know the work of the Spirit is real.

Many times I have sensed the presence of the Spirit in worship services or during church meetings of all kinds. True, I have also attended meetings where the Spirit was notably absent. The difference was astounding! The presence of the Spirit cannot be scientifically demonstrated; no photograph or videotape will record Her presence. But just as trusting faith and peace of heart are undeniable realities for those who possess these, the presence of the Spirit makes itself felt to those who welcome Her.

Quite a few times I have felt how the Spirit has guided me through difficult meetings, when I was at a loss what to say or how to proceed, but somehow found the arguments, was able to choose the right words and could remember the relevant information; when the situation seemed deadlocked, but somehow I was given the key to open the gate to mutual understanding and conflict resolution.

And last, there is that constant gentle voice that we call conscience. Life is so full of temptations, great and small. So often we are tempted to look after our own interests rather than those of others; so often there is the enticing opportunity to do something that is profitable, even though it takes some mental gymnastics to convince ourselves that it is honest; so often we are tempted to indulge ourselves in things that are neither healthy nor wholesome. (My colleagues know what I mean.) I realize that I do not always listen to the voice of the Spirit, who is constantly sensitizing my conscience. But when I do listen, I know almost instantly that I have made the right choice, and I appreciate the guidance and support that God provides me through His Spirit.

6 Creation

God is the Creator of all things, and has revealed in Scripture the authentic account of His creative activity. In six days the Lord made "the heaven and the earth" and all living things upon the earth, and rested on the seventh day of that first week. Thus He established the Sabbath as a perpetual memorial of His completed creative work. The first man and woman were made in the image of God as the crowning work of Creation, given dominion over the world, and charged with responsibility to care for it. When the world was finished, it was "very good," declaring the glory of God.

Gen. 1; 2; Exod. 20:8-11;

Ps. 19:1-6; 33:6, 9; 104;

Heb. 11:3.

Chapter 6

Creative Creatures

I would like to know how many educated Adventists—students, professionals, and even church leaders—believe in a literal Creation in six days about six thousand years ago. From my conversations with many of them, I have concluded that it must be a considerable percentage. I have talked with quite a few "ordinary" church members who do not (or who do no longer) believe in Creationism but have accepted naturalism (belief that all things came about as a result of natural law without divine intervention) lock-stock-and-barrel. These surely form only a minority, but I venture to say that there is a significant number that holds a view that is somewhere between the two extremes of solid Creationism and wholesale naturalism. Some believe in a six-day creation but allow for more time than six thousand years. Others support some form of theistic evolution (i.e., evolution that leaves room for divine involvement).

I have great sympathy for those who struggle with this issue. And I wish the church would do more in addressing it. Not only by providing more solid material that supports the traditional Adventist position but first of all by creating an atmosphere where this important topic can be discussed in a nonthreatening way. It is very difficult to say that you have questions about Creation with-

45

out jeopardizing your position in the local church, let alone as a paid worker in the church. Yet, I have to admit that through the years I have struggled with this issue. And I certainly have not solved all aspects of the problem in my own mind.

I have read quite a bit on both sides of the issue. Some Creationist books have been so convincing in shooting down the arguments in favor of evolution that I laid them down with the feeling that at last I had seen solid arguments. But a little later I would read books that dealt with the origins of the earth and of life on this planet from an evolutionist perspective, and I would be thoroughly confused because some of the arguments seem so plausible.

So where do I stand today? I have no doubt that God is the Creator. From what I have read I would certainly favor a short rather than an ultrashort chronology. In other words, the earth and life upon it have probably existed for longer than six thousand years. I feel that the Bible, and also the writings of Ellen White—as I understand them—allow for this. As to how literally I must take the Creation story, that is another matter. I believe that the Creation story is true, but that does not necessarily mean that it has to be accepted as a complete, factual report of what happened. The truth of the Creation story is presented in a literary form that is undeniably effective and powerful but is not meant to be a scientific paper.

Not being an expert in any of the exact sciences, my reasoning may be flawed. Nonetheless, let me tell you why I have become convinced that evolution as it is commonly presented (a long process leading from simple life forms to human life), is an unsatisfactory explanation of human origins. I start from the basic premise that we are moral agents and that as such we are accountable to God. Now, if life evolved over millions of years, from simple life structures to animal life to protohumans and finally to modern man, there must have been a moment where a form of animal life became a form of human life. There must have been a dividing line between amoral animals and moral human beings. Or to phrase it more theologically, between beings that were only capable of temporal life and beings that were potentially capable of eternal life; beings that could not be saved or lost and beings that could be saved or lost. To me it is difficult to see how there could have been such a transition. Did this change from an amoral nature to a moral nature occur in just one specimen or in a few protohumans en route to full humanity? Did this change take place in a gradual way, from amoral to a-little-moral to fully moral? In my own limited way I have given considerable thought to this, and even though these thoughts may seem unscientific or philosophically flawed, or whatever, this has become a strong argument for my rejection of the evolutionist view. If man is something special—a being that is responsible to God—he must be totally different from other forms of life.

More than rational reasons

Believing in God as my Creator is more than an academic matter. If the Creation story is true (in the sense I described above), I am more than a highly developed animal: I am a being created in the image of God. Whatever that means, it does imply a very special tie between God and me. Being created in the image of the Creator means that I am also a creator, albeit in a derived, and very limited, way. That idea urges me to be creative in my daily life and work.

To believe in Creation has another, most important implication. Evolution is, in final analysis, a matter of chance, whereas Creation is a matter of destiny. To believe in Creation is to affirm that God's design and power is somehow at the basis of everything, rather than fate and chance. On the personal level that means that my life has a purpose and destiny. I am not the product of blind chance, nor does my future depend on the roll of some biochemical dice.

Accepting the truth of the Creation story has yet another vital implication: I am not alone in being the product of God's creative power: so are all the people around me, and so is the flora and the fauna, the oceans and the forests, the mineral resources and the atmosphere. The charge to Adam and Eve to look after God's creation lifts concern for the environment from the realm of common sense and responsibility for our children to the sphere of religion. Having said that, I realize that my church has not done so well in emphasizing this aspect of the truth of Creation and that I myself have a long way to go in internalizing that truth, so that it truly becomes an integral part of my lifestyle.

Last, of course, the Creation story tells me that time comes in units of seven days at a time. There is a divine rhythm of six plus one that ought to be the basic pattern of human existence. Again, I know I have not taken full advantage of the blessing of the seventh-day Sabbath. But even in the imperfect way in which I "observe" the Sabbath, I regularly catch something of the divine rest that transforms and gives meaning to all my activities.

7 The Nature of Man

Man and woman were made in the image of God with individuality, the power and freedom to think and to do. Though created free beings, each is an indivisible unity of body, mind, and spirit, dependent upon God for life and breath and all else. When our first parents disobeyed God, they denied their dependence upon Him and fell from their high position under God. The image of God in them was marred, and they became subject to death. Their descendants share this fallen nature and its consequences. They are born with weaknesses and tendencies to evil. But God in Christ reconciled the world to Himself and by His Spirit restores in penitent mortals the image of their Maker. Created for the glory of God, they are called to love Him and one another, and to care for their environment.

Gen. 1:26-28; 2:7; Ps. 8:4-8; Acts 17:24-28; Gen. 3; Ps. 51:5; Rom. 5:12-17; 2 Cor. 5:19, 20; Ps. 51:10; 1 John 4:7, 8, 11, 20; Gen. 2:15.

Chapter 7

Free!

This statement about "the nature of man" contains a series of extremely significant elements.

1. We are male or female.
2. We bear the image of God.
3. We have individuality.
4. We are free to think.
5. We are free to act.
6. We are a unity of body, mind and spirit.
7. We are not what we should be.
8. We can be restored to what we ought to be.

I will focus on four of these points. My church tells me that it is part of one of its fundamental beliefs that I am a sexual being, that I am a unique individual, that I am free to think, and that I am free in what I do. It has taken me a long time to realize that this is indeed not merely an inner conviction but part of my religion. And it is not heresy—it is solid Adventist teaching!

Why has it taken me many years to discover these basic truths? Could it be that these truths have remained somewhat obscured in Adventism? The kind of Adventism that I was taught as a teenager did not tell me anything about sexuality—except that in the last days there would be widespread immorality, it emphasized conformity rather than uniqueness, and I certainly was not left with the impression that there was much latitude for individual thinking or acting.

To begin a statement about the essence of humankind by making the point that we are either male or female is highly significant. It seems to shout at the reader: Whatever else you are, you are first of all a sexual being. Gender and everything that is related to it is not something of secondary or tertiary importance. To recognize, to develop, and to enjoy your manhood or womanhood is an essential part of your humanity! And so, if I have a healthy interest in sex and enjoy my sexuality, I am on the right track. It is disturbing to see how the Adventist Church is far from immune to the cheapening of sexuality that seems to be so pervasive in today's world. But, at the same time, it is highly gratifying to notice that in recent times many church members have learned to deal with their sexuality in a much more wholesome and creative way than earlier generations of Adventists may have found possible.

Second, this statement affirms another truth that I hold very dear. I am a unique individual. Now, let me hasten to say that I realize that this is only part of the picture, because I am also part of a community. I cannot live in isolation from others, and to a considerable extent I derive my identity from the communities to which I belong. I am part of a family that extends into the past and into the future, I am a proud citizen of the country in which I was born, and I am a Seventh-day Adventist. But I am also just me. I am a unique being. Many of my friends will immediately agree and will happily provide some anecdotes to illustrate some of that uniqueness. But in all seriousness, I am unique and I do not need to hide that uniqueness. I do not have to conform to a precise precooked pattern. I can be myself and I may create a space for myself where I can be myself. That was quite a discovery: to realize that I do not have to feel guilty about this, but that this is actually embedded in one of the fundamental beliefs!

Third, the statement assures that I am expected to think for myself. I am not just to blindly accept what others tell me. I am not to simply take for granted the answers others have found. There is room for enquiry, for critical analysis, for questioning, even for doubt. Once again, I realize that there must be a balance. As created beings we must know that human thinking has its severe limitations. We must realize that often our thinking is far from straight. The apostle Paul tells us more than once that there is something seriously wrong with the unconverted mind (1 Timothy 6:5; 2 Timothy 3:8; Titus 1:15). For one thing, our thinking has the tendency to become less and less Christian and more and more secular. But having said all that, I may nonetheless conclude that I do not have to feel guilty when I do not take things for granted; when, like the Anselm, one of the great medieval theologians, I cherish a faith that seeks to understand (a *fides quaerens intellectum,* as the famous phrase says).

Unfortunately, thinking Christians—or more specifically, Adventists who think and ask hard questions—can be very lonely people. Many in this category eventually leave the church. As in most other organizations, thinking people are somewhat of a nuisance. An efficient organization needs pragmatics who get things done rather than people who constantly question things. In many Sabbath School classes difficult questions are not always appreciated. (If you want to read a good book on the topic of Christian thinking, try Harry Blamires *The Christian Mind—How Should a Christian Think?* (Servant Books, Ann Arbor, 1963); a book that is a bit dated, very Anglican, but quite useful.)

Finally, I am free in what I do. At the very core of my being I am a free agent. I have the choice to go after the good and the beautiful or to opt for the bad and the ugly. But there is much more to the Christian concept of freedom. Remember the basic premise of this book: The truth sets us free. The Christian enjoys a freedom that is foreign to those who think they are so emancipated that they need no parameters for their freedom. This freedom is not licentiousness or lawlessness. It is not a freedom to lie and cheat, to steal and to defraud, to be mean and unfaithful. But it is a freedom that allows for our personal development, it allows for a creative lifestyle, it invites us to experiment and to seek adventure. It is a freedom to worship God in whatever way I choose; a freedom to celebrate the richness of my culture; a freedom to make Sabbath keeping meaningful to me, in my specific situation; a freedom in determining which programs of the church I buy into, etc. I may claim that freedom for myself, but I must also extend it to others. Tolerance, therefore, is the collateral of this freedom.

Just one final question: Why is it that so many people in our church get so terribly upset if someone expresses some doubt regarding fundamental beliefs such as number twenty-three or number twenty-six, yet these same people seem to get away with ignoring some of the vital aspects of fundamental belief number seven?

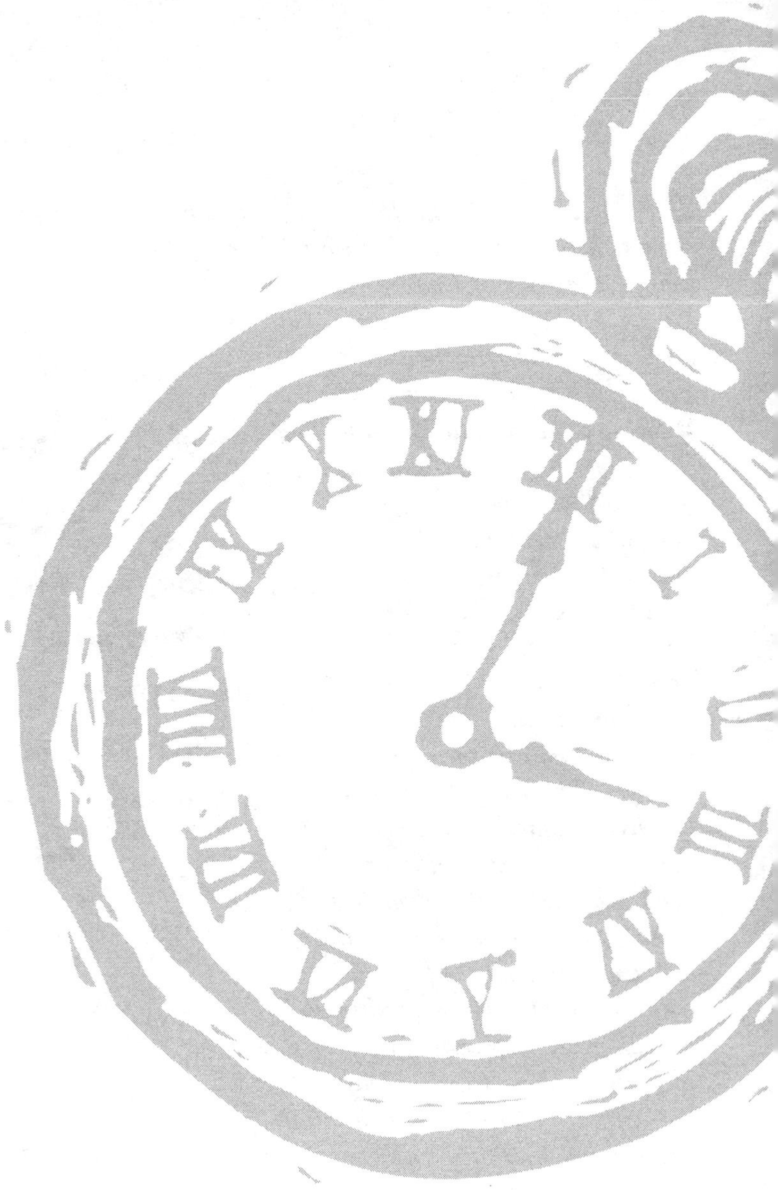

All humanity is now involved in a great controversy between Christ and Satan regarding the character of God, His law, and His sovereignty over the universe. This conflict originated in heaven when a created being, endowed with freedom of choice, in self-exaltation became Satan, God's adversary, and led into rebellion a portion of the angels. He introduced the spirit of rebellion into this world when he led Adam and Eve into sin. This human sin resulted in the distortion of the image of God in humanity, the disordering of the created world, and its eventual devastation at the time of the worldwide flood. Observed by the whole creation, this world became the arena of universal conflict, out of which the God of love will ultimately be vindicated. To assist His people in this controversy, Christ sends the Holy Spirit and the loyal angels to guide, protect, and sustain them in the way of salvation.

**Rev. 12:4-9; Isa. 14:12-14;
Ezek. 28:12-18; Gen. 3;
Rom. 1:19-32; 5:12-21;
8:19-22; Gen. 6–8;
2 Peter 3:6; 1 Cor. 4:9;
Heb. 1:14.**

Chapter 8

A Look Behind the Scenes

I always want to know what is going on. When most boys of my age were dreaming of becoming a policeofficer, a pilot, or a firefighter, I saw journalism as my destiny. Later, when I was a student at Newbold College in England, the dean of men must have noted my innate curiosity, because he assigned me a room next to the entrance of the dormitory where I could keep track of all comings and goings!

Today, many years later, my curiosity as to what is happening in the world has not disappeared. I read several daily newspapers, and there are few days when I do not spend some time with the BBC, Sky News, and CNN. And when it comes to the church, I gather my news both from the official sources and through the grapevine.

Naturally, my desire to know what is happening where I live and elsewhere in the world does not stop with national and international news. As a Christian I cannot avoid the question: Where is God in all this? I have no problem thanking Him for the good things that happen. But most of the news is about war, disasters, terrorism, crime, accidents, and scandals. Where is God in all this? I know He is supposed to be in control of everything. But how do I reconcile that idea with the carnage of the civil wars in various corners of the earth? How can I see His love in the pictures of refugee camps and the images of destruction after a hurricane has torn a deadly path through a suburban neighborhood or a drunk driver has killed a mother of four young children? How does a caring God fit in with the depletion of the ozone layer and ever-recurring murderous floods?

Many theologians and writers much brighter than I have tried to deal with the problem of evil. Sometimes they make sense, sometimes they just muddle the issue further. But, in the final analysis, there is no fully satisfying answer. We cannot fathom the mystery of evil. We will never truly understand how sin could originate in a perfect universe, just as we can never fully comprehend the endless love of God, who paid the ultimate price to deal with the sin problem. And surely, when we consider God's sublime solution for the sin problem, we lose the right to question His wisdom for handling it the way He has chosen to.

Nonetheless, we are allowed a glimpse behind the scenes. A careful reading of the Bible allows us to make a number of deductions as to what is happening. This will not answer all questions. But it does give us a background for understanding history, past and present, a little better. It provides us with a philosophy of history that helps us to see some broad outlines.

The big picture

Adventists have developed the concept of the "great controversy." They reject the notion that history is subject to endless cycles; they just as firmly reject any materialistic philosophy of history. It is not just chance or evolution or economic forces that determine the course of world events. The history of this world is part of a greater drama: the great controversy between Christ and Satan, the eternal struggle between right and wrong, love and hate, life and death.

How does knowing all this help me? First, it gives me a perspective on things. What has happened in the past and what is happening today is all part of a larger fabric. As a curious human being, I find satisfaction in knowing about this underlying pattern of things. It helps me in my reading and thinking about history and in coming to grips with what I see when I turn on the nine o'clock news. And, second, it gives me a sense of involvement. This "great controversy" is not just between powers that have nothing to do with me. I am a party in the conflict. I must take sides. What I choose to do with my life is not just my own business. It is part of a vastly greater picture. Or, to put it in other words, the concept of "the great controversy" touches me not primarily on the cognitive level but on the existential level. It transcends any curiosity or intellectual inquisitiveness. It makes clear where I stand in life: I live my life either on God's side or on the enemy's side. And that makes all the difference.

9 | The Life, Death, and Resurrection of Christ

In Christ's life of perfect obedience to God's will, His suffering, death and resurrection, God provided the only means of atonement for human sin, so that those who by faith accept this atonement may have eternal life, and the whole creation may better understand the infinite and holy love of the Creator. The perfect atonement vindicates the righteousness of God's law and the graciousness of His character; for it both condemns our sin and provides for our forgiveness. The death of Christ is substitutionary and expiatory, reconciling and transforming. The resurrection of Christ proclaims God's triumph over the forces of evil, and for those who accept the atonement assures their final victory over sin and death. It declares the Lordship of Jesus Christ, before whom every knee in heaven and on earth will bow.

John 3:16; Isa. 53;

1 Peter 2:21, 22;

1 Cor. 15:3, 4, 20-22;

2 Cor. 5:14, 15, 19-21;

Rom. 1:4; 3:25; 4:25; 8:3, 4;

1 John 2:2; 4:10; Col. 2:15;

Phil. 2:6-11.

Chapter 9

He Knows How Much I Can Take

If you keep your ear to the ground and try to stay abreast of theological trends in the Adventist Church, you must have heard of the "moral influence" theory. The proponents of that theory believe that we become changed as we contemplate the sacrificial death of Jesus on the cross and that therein lies the essence of the atonement. I have no quarrel with the first part of that statement. Of course, a confrontation with infinite love and compassion and with the willingness to suffer an ignominious death for a good cause can leave only the most hardened of individuals untouched. Indeed, we cannot help but be deeply affected by regularly reflecting on that sublime example of unselfish love. But I am deeply convinced that Christ's atonement should not be reduced to this one aspect.

Having said that, however, I am also convinced that those who speak about Christ's death only in terms of a legal transaction or of substitution do not do justice to what Christ did for us on the cross either. The Bible uses a variety of metaphors to describe Christ's atoning death; none is meant to be the last word; in fact, there is no final word. Human words will simply never adequately express by what process God became reconciled to man. It was "in Christ," and that is all we know and in fact all that matters. His death brought life. Surely His death still does a great deal for us, as we meditate on it, but only because His sacrifice on Calvary did something for us that nothing else could have done. My faith is ultimately not based on my experience, however important that may be, but on an irreversible, incomparable divine act. My sin problem has been dealt with once and for all. But it came at a cost. The highest possible cost. The life of the Son of God.

A few years ago, while on a visit to America, I saw during one of my rather frequent stops at bookstores a book with a fascinating title. I had never heard of the author and had no idea that years later it would still be among the top ten bestsellers on the New York Times list. I am referring to Dr. M. Scott Peck's book *The Road Less Traveled*. Some people have warned me about New Age philosophies in the book. Well, I can see how one might come to that conclusion by reading some of his later books, but I did not detect any of that in this book that by now has sold over five million copies in the United States alone. The book has a powerful message: Life is not easy. But you can only grow if you accept life's difficulties and deal with them, rather than avoid them. Dr. Peck invites his readers to take "the road less traveled" that has its bumps and potholes but will eventually lead to the right destination.

Many of us prefer a smooth road through life, the busy road that most people take. We have a tendency to avoid difficulties and sacrifice. Even in our daily professional lives we tend to deal with the easy things first and leave the difficult jobs till later. Often that means that these are not dealt with at all. And when it comes to personal problems profoundly affecting our own life and that of others around us, we must admit that we often run away from them. Making real sacrifices that cost us dearly . . . well, that is another story altogether.

I do not at all support the "moral influence theory" of the atonement, but I realize that Christ's willingness to go the "road less traveled" must also motivate and enable me to take that route through life. Writing these lines, I cannot get away from the question: How well do I do in facing difficulties, or to put it more bluntly, in bringing sacrifices? That is a discomforting question to answer.

The Bible is full of stories of people who truly sacrificed, often in terms of their own life. Few if any of the apostles died a natural death. They paid for their loyalty to Christ with their lives. And just think of what the apostle Paul had to go through! Thank God, I have never had to face persecution for my faith. I have been insulted because of my religious convictions, but I have never been beaten up, or worse, because I am an Adventist Christian. Some of my brethren will be quick to add: Just wait for what will happen in the future. They point to the end-time scenario—the time of trouble and the seven last plagues. When things get hot, they say, it will remain to be seen whether you are able to endure. Indeed, will I be willing (and able) to suffer physical pain, torture, or even death rather than deny Christ? I hope so; that is all I can say.

What kind of sacrifices am I willing to make? If I could save the lives of my wife or of my children, knowing that it would cost my own life, would I do that? Of course this remains an academic problem until such a concrete situation arises. But yes, maybe, I would bring that sacrifice. But would I also do it for one of my sisters, for some friend, for a colleague? Quite frankly, I do not know, but I doubt it. And for a total stranger? I don't think so.

What about sacrifices on a lower level? Yes, I am willing to sacrifice some of my time and some of my money. I am at times willing to go to some trouble to help people, even if it is inconvenient. I went with my family to Africa, where we served as missionaries for over six years. The first two years in particular presented many challenges. That should qualify as a considerable sacrifice, some would say. It was in some ways. But we never were in any greater danger than we would have been in Europe. We never had any problem in finding the kind of food we liked. Our house was larger than the one we presently have in England. We were able to employ a servant to do most of the housework. That certainly is beyond our means in England. The only real sacrifice probably consisted of the fact that for most of the time our children were not with us and that we were so far away from relatives and friends. (Maybe there was one other sacrifice: There was no good book shop where I could browse on a regular basis). But all-in-all, how much did I really sacrifice?

God knows how much I can take, and it seems that He has graciously kept the amount of sacrifice He expects me to bring to a minimum. He sees that I am not very good in bringing sacrifices and has so far shielded me from difficulties that I would not be able to handle. But I realize that one day there may be a real bump in the road; there may very well soon come a moment when I will have to pay a heavy price for the sake of someone or something dear to me. I had better focus my attention more resolutely on the sacrifice of my Lord. That will be the source of strength and inspiration as I continue on my "road less traveled."

In infinite love and mercy God made Christ, who knew no sin, to be sin for us, so that in Him we might be made the righteousness of God. Led by the Holy Spirit we sense our need, acknowledge our sinfulness, repent of our transgressions, and exercise faith in Jesus as Lord and Christ, as Substitute and Example. This faith which receives salvation comes through the divine power of the Word and is the gift of God's grace. Through Christ we are justified, adopted as God's sons and daughters, and delivered from the lordship of sin. Through the Spirit we are born again and sanctified; the Spirit renews our minds, writes God's law of love in our hearts, and we are given the power to live a holy life. Abiding in Him we become partakers of the divine nature and have the assurance of salvation now and in the judgment.

2 Cor. 5:17-21; John 3:16;

Gal. 1:4; 4:4-7; Titus 3:3-7;

John 16:8; Gal. 3:13, 14;

1Peter 2:21, 22; Rom. 10:17;

Luke 17:5; Mark 9:23, 24;

Eph. 2:5-10; Rom. 3:21-26;

Col. 1:13, 14;

Rom. 8:14-17;

Gal. 3:26; John 3:3-8;

1 Peter 1:23;

Rom. 12:2;

Heb. 8:7-12;

Eze. 36:25-27; 2 Peter 1:3, 4;

Rom. 8:1-4; 5:6-10.

Chapter 10

Having Regrets Without Feeling Guilty

I suppose I am a reasonably decent person. The only time I ever had to appear in court was when I had forgotten to pay a fine for illegal parking. Hearing and deciding my case took the judge about seven minutes, and he actually made me pay less than the amount of the original ticket. I can truthfully say that I have no criminal record. I have never been arrested and have never been in jail. I have never stolen a car or engaged in shoplifting. I have never been in trouble with "the law" in any of the five different countries where I have lived.

And I suppose I also have a pretty good track record when it comes to the heinous sins referred to in the Ten Commandments. I am not into idol worship, make no habit of swearing, do not wash my car on Sabbath (actually, I do not wash my car very often on any other day of the week either), I have never killed or injured another person, I have never had a mistress or used the services of a call-girl, and I believe I am not really envious of other people's houses or Mercedeses.

But I have read enough in the Bible, and my conscience functions well enough, to know that this is a very superficial way of looking at myself. I realize how true Christ's words are: External actions are only a very small part of the story. He points to our

67

motives as just as important or even more important than our actual deeds. He tells us that hating someone is just as bad as killing someone. And that looking "with a lustful eye" at a woman is not much different from the act of adultery. When I look at myself from that perspective, things begin to appear a little less comfortable. But still I can feel reasonably good about myself. I am not oblivious to female beauty, but I have no wild fantasies when I meet an attractive woman. And although it is true that I find some people a lot easier to get along with than others and although there are some people who tax my patience, I do not really hate anyone.

Yet I know myself well enough to realize that I have made more than my share of mistakes. There are many things in my past I wish I could undo. There are things I have said to people who are no longer alive that I wish I had never said. I have hurt people in many ways. Some of the occasions where that happened I remember quite vividly, but there are no doubt many other instances that I am not even aware of. I love my wife and children, but I know that I have not always been a perfect husband and father. I can be quite inconsiderate and short-fused. I can be quite selfish and at times tend to pursue my own interests and plans, without giving due attention to the feelings and opinions of those around me.

What is sin?

When we study the biblical concept of sin, we find that the original languages used several words with different shades of meaning. These words describe sin as rebellion against God, as going our own way, as breaking the divine law. But they also emphasize that sin is: not reaching our full potential, leaving things undone that should have been done, missing the mark. When I apply that kind of definition of sin to my life, I have very little reason to be proud. So many words I should have said have been left unspoken. So many occasions where I could have helped others, where I could have made a difference, have been selfishly ignored. So many chances to improve my skills, to learn, to develop and grow have been left unused. So many things could have been accomplished but never were because I lacked the initiative, the courage, or the willpower to do so. I can look back on some successes in my personal life, my relationship with others, and my work, but the list of failures, for which I have to take at least part of the blame, is quite disheartening.

If my faith in Christ means anything at all, it must—and does— make the difference in dealing with these feelings of imperfection, failure, and guilt. This whole sin-and-guilt-complex that results from an honest self-inventory is taken care of. Sure, I have my regrets, and I sometimes kick myself for having done certain things and for having ignored other things. But I do not go through life with a burden of guilt that gets heavier by the day as I make new mistakes and fail to do what I ought to have done. I have what is usually called "the assurance of salvation." That does indeed take a load off my shoulders. It does indeed bring a marvelous sense of freedom. I am a sinner. I have always been one and will remain so as long as I live. But Christ knows how to deal with sinners because He has dealt with sin—not only with "sin" in a general way but with my sins: with every one of them.

11 The Church

The church is the community of believers who
confess Jesus Christ as Lord and Saviour. In
our continuity with the people of God in
Old Testament times, we are called
out from the world; and we join
together for worship, for fellowship, for instruction in the Word,
for the celebration of the Lord's
Supper, for service to all
mankind, and for the worldwide proclamation of the
gospel. The church derives its
authority from Christ, who
is the Incarnate Word, and
from the Scriptures, which
are the written Word. The
church is God's family; adopted by Him as children, its
members live on the basis of the
new covenant. The church is the
body of Christ, a community of
faith of which Christ Himself is the
Head. The church is the bride for
whom Christ died that He might sanc-
tify and cleanse her. At His return in triumph, He will present her to Himself a glorious church, the faithful of all the ages, the purchase of His blood, not having spot or wrinkle, but holy
and without blemish.

Gen. 12:3; Acts 7:38;

Eph. 4:11-15; 3:8-11;

Matt. 28:19, 20; 16:13-20;

18:18; Eph. 2:19-22; 1:22,

23; 5:23-27; Col. 1:17, 18.

Chapter 11

Thank God: Its Future Does Not Depend on Me

How important is the church to me? If I had to give an answer to that question by putting a mark on a scale from one to ten (one being not important at all and ten signifying ultimate importance), my pen would no doubt move toward the highest number. I have been working for the church for more than thirty years. It has been quite an interesting time. Most of that time I have been extremely busy. (But I should not complain; I am a workaholic and would probably have worked just as hard in any other job.) Most of the time has been extremely interesting. The work has usually been challenging. I happen to like a fair bit of traveling, and my various assignments have given me plenty of opportunity for that. The church has faithfully paid my salary. I have not become rich, but the financial rewards have not been quite as bad as some church employees claim they are. My social life largely revolves around the church. It is no exaggeration to say that the church is my life.

But that is not what this fundamental belief is about. I work for the church. But do I also belong to the church? Do I truly feel part of that community that calls itself the body of Christ? Do I enjoy worshiping with others? Do I truly recognize other believers as my "brothers" and "sisters"? Do I feel enriched when I have been together with them, and do I contribute to the functioning of the church body, not from a sense of duty but as a genuine joy?

Let me be honest: I have some problems with these questions. I often wish my local church would be a bit more exciting and that the church service would "give" me more. I often wish the sermons were more relevant to the many questions I have. And sometimes I wonder whether I would be just as faithful a church attender if I were not employed by the church and if I would feel less obliged to set a good example. And believe me, I know quite a few church leaders who have shared similar feelings with me. But although the church services at times leave me unsatisfied, I realize that my Christian experience would be seriously jeopardized if I did not go to church and did not actively participate in corporate worship.

I have a long wish list of things that I would like to see changed in my church. I am committed to helping to bring about some change, slowly but surely. I believe in the value of tradition, but I also am utterly convinced that the church must be a living body that changes and grows and matures. And I know that I must be involved, not only on the professional level but on the personal level, as a member among other members and that I must foster an attitude that is not primarily focused on receiving but rather on giving and sharing.

The church of the future

I often worry about the future of the church. Will the church remain united, or will we be torn apart by the conflicting agendas of liberals and conservatives? Can we survive all the nationalistic and ethnic tensions that undeniably put up their ugly heads? Will our current model of church organization continue to serve us well as we enter the twenty-first century?

The church is growing rapidly in many areas of the world. But have we lost the momentum in the western world? I cannot help but think of the claims made by historians of religion that religious movements go through a number of phases but are eventually doomed to extinction. Are we in the western world, in particular among the Caucasians, witnessing the beginning of the end of Adventism? Is the lack of enthusiasm among our youth to join the religion of their parents a telling sign that Adventism is on the way out? Does not the minimal success of recruiting new members among whites in the secular West point in the same direction?

These and many similar thoughts do not easily disappear. But when I look at this "fundamental belief" about the church, I am reminded that the present lack of success in some parts of the world should not take away our hope and our assurance that all will be well in the end: "At his return in triumph, He [Christ] will present her [the church] to Himself a glorious church, the faithful of all the ages, the purchase of his blood, not having spot or wrinkle, but holy and without blemis." (Fundamental belief number 11). That statement can be substantiated by abundant biblical proof, and that should set my mind at rest about the ultimate outcome of the history of God's church. And in the meantime I have the privilege to keep working in and for the church in a part of the world that admittedly is hitting a bit of rough weather. Reason for worry? Certainly. A challenge to find new ways of reaching people, of reclaiming people who have left, of keeping people inside the flock when they are tempted to wander away, certainly. But no reason for despair. For it is not me or us or our efforts that will determine whether the church has a future. It is the Head of the church who will make sure that the church is there when He comes to take it home.

12 The Remnant and Its Mission

The universal church is composed of all who truly believe in Christ, but in the last days, a time of widespread apostasy, a remnant has been called out to keep the commandments of God and the faith of Jesus. This remnant announces the arrival of the judgment hour, proclaims salvation through Christ, and heralds the approach of His second advent. This proclamation is symbolized by the three angels of Revelation 14; it coincides with the work of judgment in heaven and results in a work of repentance and reform on earth. Every believer is called to have a personal part in this worldwide witness.

Rev. 12:17; 14:6-12; 18:1-4; 2 Cor. 5:10; Jude 3, 14; 1 Peter 1:16-19; 2 Peter 3:10-14; Rev. 21:1-14.

Chapter 12

A Remnant of 50 Million?

During a recent meeting at the General Conference headquarters one of the leaders of our church told the delegates from around the world that by the year 2020 the Seventh-day Adventist Church might have 50,000,000 members. Of course, the speaker was aware of at least two assumptions: (1) that Christ's coming would not take place before that time; (2) that accessions of new members would continue at the present rate.

The Adventist Church worldwide is growing into a body of respectable size. I still remember the time when we had less than one million members. Today we are nearing the ten million mark. Fifteen years ago a baptismal goal of 1,000 new adherents per day seemed almost preposterous. Today about 2,000 new Adventists swell our ranks every day.

What does that do to our theology? Have we not always believed that the advent movement was to be God's small remnant, the "few" that would be saved, over and against the masses that would be lost? Was this remnant not identical with the 144,000 of Revelation 7? Those who are familiar with the development of Adventist teachings know that at first 144,000 was regarded as a literal number. When the Adventist Church began to grow and the membership increased beyond 144,000, uneasiness began to set in.

Of course, there was going to be a final "sifting," and not all who were on the books of the Adventist Church were going to make it in the final test. But as the church increased in size, more and more Adventist ministers were beginning to argue that 144,000 was not a literal but a symbolic number, so that a larger number of believers could be accommodated.

Nonetheless, Adventist publications continued to emphasize that there was going to be but a small remnant. Only relatively few would choose to identify with God's "last church" and would remain loyal. And that is still firmly embedded in our end-time scenario.

Yet there has always been another element. We have always maintained that God's Spirit would be poured out in a "latter rain" with wonderful results. In my mind this produces a tension that I have never totally resolved: the contrast between the lack of response to the preaching of the Adventist message and the expected reversal of our limited success.

Today I sense this tension even more strongly than I did some years ago. On the one hand, I continue to read in our Adventist literature about the small "remnant"; I know about the statement that there will be hardly any faith left on earth, and at the same time I hear our triumphalist statements about the unprecedented growth we are experiencing in many lands and predictions about even greater numerical strength in the next few decades.

Yet somehow I believe this tension is healthy and justified. For the Bible clearly points to this final controversy between the "few" and the "many." The Bible does not allow for the wishful thinking of many theologians of past and present (and the idea is very popular among theologians today!) that eventually all people will be saved. Unfortunately, many will be lost, not because God did not try to save them but because they themselves, in spite of all divine initiatives on their behalf, deliberately decided to say No to the offer of salvation.

But having said that, we must hasten to add that there will be a rich "harvest." Revelation 7 not only refers to the 144,000 but also to the great multitude of the saved that no one can number. I know that traditionally most Adventist commentators have explained this chapter as referring to two different categories of people: The 144,000 stand for the loyal "remnant" that lives to see Christ come, while the "great multitude" describes the believers of all ages who are resurrected when Christ comes. I find it increasingly attractive to think of the two groups as referring to the same people, from two different perspectives. The 144,000-perspective reminds me of the fact that not all will be saved, while the "great multitude"-perspective holds the promise that God's plan of salvation will ultimately be proven to be very successful.

But even if this "two-perspectives view" is incorrect, I still believe there is ample reason to think of the remnant as surprisingly large! The number 144,000 is built on two key constituents: twelve and ten. Twelve is a number that stands for God's people (think of the twelve tribes in the Old Testament and the twelve apostles as the founders of the New Testament church), while ten stands for completeness. 10x10x10 (1,000) emphasizes this element of completeness beyond any possible doubt. God will make sure that all who are His will make it! That is the point we should never forget. The remnant concept is not meant to make us depressed and to fill us with anxiety: If so few will be accepted, if it is so difficult to belong to the happy few who will ultimately be saved, where does that leave me? How can I hope to be among that tiny group of superspiritual giants? No, the remnant concept is good news. It tells us that those who want to be with God are safe. He has the resources to pull us through, all of us who have committed ourselves to Him.

All speculation about how small or large the remnant will be is rather futile. And, by the way, the strict identification of the Seventh-day Adventist Church as we know it today with the biblical remnant may be a bit too easy. There are just too many among us who are Adventist without being Christian, and there are just too many genuine Christians elsewhere who have not (yet?) joined our ranks, to simply assume that being an Adventist and being part of the remnant are one and the same thing.

Yet I believe there are solid reasons for belonging to the Adventist Church and for seeing some definite linkage between my church and the biblical remnant. These reasons do not exclusively, or even primarily, have to do with any idea that being an Adventist assures me of a greater chance of salvation. Yes, as an Adventist I have a better idea than most people of the times in which we live. I have a better understanding of the ongoing battle between the forces of good and evil that form the backdrop of past and present. I have a better understanding than the vast majority of people of what is at stake and what the biblical implications are of being a follower of Christ. Therefore, belonging to this special group of people—to this "remnant," to use the biblical term—provides me with a definite sense of mission. It does not mean that I am right in everything and that adherents of other world religions, let alone other Christians, are totally wrong in everything they believe and do—that I belong to the relatively small group that will be saved, while all others will be lost. It does not (unfortunately) even mean that I belong to a group of people that on the average is more spiritual and more dedicated than any other religious body. But it does mean that I am privileged to be part of a force that God wants to use in a very special way to communicate to this world some specific aspects of the gospel message that must be heard. To be a part of such a mission is both an awesome responsibility and a wonderful privilege.

13 Unity in the Body of Christ

The church is one body with many members, called from every nation, kindred, tongue, and people. In Christ we are a new creation; distinctions of race, culture, learning, and nationality, and difference between high and low, rich and poor, male and female must not be divisive among us. We are all equal in Christ, who by one Spirit has bonded us into one fellowship with Him and with one another; we are to serve and be served without partiality or reservation. Through the revelation of Jesus Christ in the Scriptures we share the same faith and hope, and reach out in one witness to all. This unity has its source in the oneness of the triune God, who has adopted us as His children.

Rom. 12:4, 5; 1 Cor. 12:12-14;

Matt. 28:19, 20; Ps. 133:1, 2;

2 Cor. 5:16, 17; Acts 17:26, 27;

Gal. 3:27, 29; Col. 3:10-15;

Eph. 4:14-16; 4:1-6;

John 17:20-23.

Chapter 13

I don't often buy a book just because it has an intriguing title. But when I saw a book in the sociology section of a large book shop with the title *The McDonaldization of Society*, I couldn't resist it. The subtitle "An Investigation Into the Changing Character of Contemporary Social Life" indicates that this presumably is a serious sociological study. The reader learns lots of interesting facts about the famous, worldwide, ever-expanding fast-food chain. In the United States there is now one McDonald's restaurant for every 2,250 Americans. A raw hamburger weighs exactly 1.6 ounces. A precooked hamburger measures precisely 3.875 inches across. It contain a maximum of 19 percent fat. A hamburger bun is exactly 3.5 inches in diameter. If you want to know more about the measurements and ingredients of the Big Mac or McChicken, you will have to buy the book yourself. I am referring to the book for another reason. It emphasizes the predictability factor as one of the main reasons behind the enormous success of this restaurant chain. Wherever you go, you see the Golden Arches. (A recent study indicated that in some Western European countries most people more readily understand the meaning of the McDonald's symbol than that of the Christian cross!) Whether you visit a McDonald's in the USA, in Britain, in South Africa, or in Warsaw, the hamburgers taste exactly the same (and, fortunately, so do the milkshakes!). The book then gives scores of examples of other international chains that build their success on this same principle of complete uniformity. They develop a successful formula and they stick with it, everywhere!

Is that what you expect of your church? Do you want your church to look the same and be the same all around the world? Do you want a church that not only believes the same wherever you go but also adheres to the same calendar of events, follows the same organizational procedures, uses the same kind of music and the same worship patterns; a church that, wherever you go, has the same books, runs the same Daniel and Revelation Seminars and the same Stop-Smoking Clinics, and eats the same kind of soy sausages? If that is your ideal for the church, you are going to be increasingly disappointed. This kind of McDonaldization of the church does not appeal to me at all. My ideal of the church is not one with strict uniformity but one where a fundamental unity expresses itself in a wide cultural diversity.

Whether we like it or not, modern Adventism displays an increasing pluriformity. There is a variety in worship styles, in standards of behavior, and even in beliefs (I will come back to that last aspect). Many feel that this trend toward greater pluriformity endangers the unity of the church. Others, like me, are happy with this development: People with different cultures should have space to make their religion relevant to their situation. Only if that happens can the church be truly their church, rather than a foreign religious body that offers a set of doctrinal truths to which they subscribe with their minds while the rest of their being remains largely untouched. Multiculturalism is to be embraced not because it is inevitable but because it gives expression to God's new creation in its fullness.

Of course, extremes must, as usual, be avoided. Forcing one

mode of acting and thinking upon the worldwide church would require a totalitarian monocultural approach that is doomed to fail in the long run. On the other hand, cultural diversity must never be understood in terms of total relativism. All cultures must be judged by the gospel. All cultures have elements that can be embraced but also elements that must be rejected!

As I read it, Fundamental Belief number thirteen squarely supports the above view. But it does make at least two other important points. 1. The many differences must never be divisive; there must be an underlying unity. 2. Whatever our differences, we have the same faith and the same hope.

This first point—the need for unity in spite of all diversity—presupposes an openness toward other cultures, a willingness to learn, and a basic attitude of interest in and appreciation for what is "different." And, more than anything else, it presupposes an attitude of tolerance! A greater measure of tolerance certainly would be on my list of things I would wish for my church. And, deep down, most of us know that this is an area where we will have to improve. Many of us will just have to keep on reminding ourselves that multiculturalism in the church is not something to be tolerated but to be celebrated. John the Revelator pictures the saints as coming from every tribe, language, and ethnic background (Revelation 5:9, 10). With their widely diverse cultures they will add to the colorful mosaic of the New Jerusalem (Revelation 21:26). If that is going to be the picture of heaven, we had better begin to appreciate it here.

The second point is just as vital: We must be bound together by the same faith and the same hope. We must agree on a basic platform of truth. For that reason we have our statement of twenty-seven Fundamental Beliefs. These are the things we hold in common. The church will soon lose its inner cohesiveness if one-half of the church keeps the Sabbath while the other half adopts Sunday as the day of worship, when some local churches admit members by sprinkling while others continue to insist on complete immersion, or when some maintain that our soul goes to heaven as soon as we die while others believe that we "know nothing" until the day of the resurrection.

But I am convinced that we must allow for a firm measure of creative tension between, on the one hand, this need for a "body of truth"—the same faith and the same hope—that unified us and the need for open discussion and a need for different approaches in our continuing search for a deeper understanding of the message of the Bible. We cannot deny that the questions people ask differ from culture to culture. In order to be relevant, Adventist theology must always be "present truth," whether one lives in Western Europe or West Africa, in the USA or in the Ukraine. Adventist theology must not only address white Anglo-Saxon concerns but also those of Afro-Americans, Asians, Africans, and Polynesians. It must speak the language of the elderly Adventist in Michigan but also the jargon of the secularized Adventist adolescent in Copenhagen. True unity is not destroyed but enriched by a willingness to listen to each other and learn from each other. The mystery of God and His self-disclosure is so rich that no one person, no generation, no one ethnic group can ever claim to have fully understood all its implications.

What is true for others is true for me: My firm convictions and theological views, however brilliant I may, in moments of self-delusion, think they are, are just that: convictions and views but never the full truth in all its supernatural splendor. In practice, I must be as willing to listen to others as I expect them to be to listen to me.

14 Baptism

By baptism we confess our faith in the death and resurrection of Jesus Christ, and testify of our death to sin and of our purpose to walk in newness of life. Thus we acknowledge Christ as Lord and Saviour, become His people, and are received as members by His church. Baptism is a symbol of our union with Christ, the forgiveness of our sins, and our reception of the Holy Spirit. It is by immersion in water and is contingent on an affirmation of faith in Jesus and evidence of repentance of sin. It follows instruction in the Holy Scriptures and acceptance of their teachings.

Rom. 6:1-6; Col. 2:12, 13; Acts 16:30-33; 22:16; 2:38; Matt. 28:19, 20.

Chapter 14

Promises Are for Real

In the early seventies an international congress sponsored by the Adventist Church was held in Amsterdam. Somehow I got heavily involved with the communications aspect of the event. One of the General Conference leaders expressed his appreciation for my hard work and promised that he would give me the grand tour of Washington if I would ever visit the American capital. I should just call him, and he would take the time to show me around. Well, in those days a low-echelon church worker in Europe did not get much of a chance to visit America. But, surprisingly enough, five or six years later I did cross the ocean on church business, and en route to my onward destination I visited the General Conference headquarters, then in Takoma Park. But I had only been minutes in the building when suddenly the person who had made that promise emerged from one of the countless offices. Recognizing me, he said, "Good to see you. Can I show you Washington? Are you free tomorrow?" I was. And I had a superb day. I continue to have high regards for my Washington guide and always pop into his office when I visit the church's headquarters. I will always see him as a prime example of people who keep their promises.

Of course, there is a different category of promises that is far more important: promises made for life. In our Western world one-third to one-half of all those who solemnly utter the words "I do" end up not doing what they promised. Every divorce, each broken home, every one-parent family is sad evidence that a large percentage of wedding vows are not kept.

I try to be sympathetic when someone's marriage breaks up. Sometimes you have seen it coming for a long time and are just surprised it did not happen earlier. In other cases you are simply baffled: You thought they were a perfect match and were totally happy! I am extremely grateful that my marriage has now lasted for more than thirty years. I just cannot imagine that my wife would decide to leave me (even though I appreciate it takes quite a bit of grace to live with me) and, likewise, I cannot imagine that I would walk away from my marriage or be unfaithful. That is not to say that there is never a ripple in our relationship nor that there is never a temptation. I have traveled extensively, in particular during the past ten years. If I were to calculate how much time I have spent away from home during these past ten years, I would guess between two and three years. And believe me, you cannot spend more than two years in hotel rooms in Africa and Europe (where most of my travel has been) without at least occasionally feeling lonely. And there have been ample opportunities for extramarital activities. But I can honestly say that these temptations have never been overwhelming, and I pray that they never will be. I love my wife, and it would cause her immense grief if I were unfaithful. I once promised to be faithful, and I intend to keep that promise. And if there is ever going to be an overwhelming temptation, I believe that this promise will reverberate in my mind and will give me strength to withstand it.

Promises to God

Baptism has a profound meaning. Being immersed signifies an identification with Christ in His death and resurrection. It is a powerful statement about ending one kind of life and beginning a new life in Christ. Read Ephesians 6 if you want to be reminded of the significance of baptism. Unfortunately, not all of us have experienced our baptism in such dramatic terms. Let's face it: A new life means something different to a criminal who has turned his back on a life of robbing banks than to a teenager who grows up in an

Adventist home and gets baptized at the age of fourteen.

I belong to that latter category. I cannot say that it was not my own desire and decision to be baptized, but there was certainly a fair amount of subtle (and even not so subtle) pressure from the pastor who preferred to have at least two baptismal candidates for the service he had planned. My baptism definitely meant something to me, but it was not the kind of watershed between two modes of existence that some people experience. It was rather a matter of continuing on the same path, of affirming my willingness to stay with what I had imbibed at home. My baptism did not keep me from experimenting with "worldly" things. It did not safeguard me against straying from the "narrow" road from time to time, against doing things that I have later regretted.

However, in retrospect, I believe my baptism has been an important factor in not getting completely away from God and the church. There was always the realization that I had made a promise and that promises must be kept! Once you make a decision, you have to stand by it, unless of course you have become convinced that you made a wrong decision. But you should not walk away from your decision because of weakness or indifference. I believe that having made the promise at an early age has helped me to re-focus again and again on God and the implications of my faith in Him for my life. My baptism always remained a reference point when things were difficult or got out of hand.

Let me add one more point: In my adolescent years I at times wondered whether I needed rebaptism, as a reaffirmation that from now onwards I would be really serious about my faith. I am glad I never fully pursued this. In final analysis, baptism and the new life have to do with God's grace, not with our input. If that were not so, I would even now need to be rebaptized on at least a weekly basis.

15 The Lord's Supper

The Lord's Supper is a participation in the emblems of the body and blood of Jesus as an expression of faith in Him, our Lord and Saviour. In this experience of communion Christ is present to meet and strengthen His people. As we partake, we joyfully proclaim the Lord's death until He comes again. Preparation for the Supper includes self-examination, repentance, and confession. The Master ordained the service of foot washing to signify renewed cleansing, to express a willingness to serve one another in Christlike humility, and to unite our hearts in love. The communion service is open to all believing Christians.

1 Cor. 10:16, 17; 11:23-30;

Matt. 26:17-30; Rev. 3:20;

John 6:48-63; 13:1-17.

Chapter 15

The Challenge of Servant-Leadership

In recent years I have sensed more and more the importance of one particular aspect of worship: the Communion service. I admit that there have been times in the past when I undervalued this quarterly event. For a long time I often felt somewhat uneasy when I participated in the Lord's Supper. I never quite managed to forget the warning I had heard so often in my younger years that it is possible to eat and drink in such a way that God would condemn me rather than bless me. Somehow that fear is no longer there. I have come to the point where I can look forward to the Communion service. I am fully convinced of the power of words but increasingly recognize the power of symbols. The Communion service with its symbols of bread and wine convey, clearer than any sermon ever could, that something unique and awesome has happened that takes care of my sin problem; that somehow Christ's suffering and death bring a wholeness to my human, imperfect existence that is beyond words.

My earlier uneasiness about the Lord's Supper probably also had to do with the foot washing that precedes it. It was not that I had no interest in the foot-washing ritual. In fact, in my senior year in college I wrote a paper on the history of foot washing. Among other things, I found it fascinating to discover how certain groups in the

Netherlands practiced foot washing in connection with the Lord's Supper until well into the nineteenth century. My first more or less scholarly article was on that very subject. I still have a few copies of the issue of the July 1966 issue of *Ministry* in which it appeared.

But although foot washing interested me as a historical phenomenon, for a long time I felt more than a little awkward with regard to its actual practice. But in the course of time I have become more appreciative of the "service of humility" as I have increasingly become aware of its meaning and have more and more realized that I can well use a good dose of humility and that this aspect of the Communion service helps me to realize that belonging to the church, and working for the church, must be a matter of true servanthood before anything else.

I have been much impressed by the book by Robert K. Greenleaf, *Servant Leadership*, which I first came across in early 1996, although it was published (by the Paulist Press) as early as in 1977. Greenleaf developed his theory of servant leadership while an executive at AT&T and subsequently a professor at such famous institutions as the Massachusetts Institute of Technology and the Harvard Business School. The concept came to him while reading Herman Hesse's novel *Journey to the East*, in which Leo, the menial servant of a group of travelers, turns out to be the true leader. The moral principle which Greenleaf draws from this is that "the great leader is seen as the servant first." He emphasizes that true leadership is not primarily a matter of managing people, let alone manipulating them. (Both words, interestingly enough, are derived from the Latin word *manus*—hand—and suggest a handling of people like commodities.) The words of Christ in Mark 10:42-45 enunciate that principle in the clearest possible way: "You know that those who are regarded as rulers of the Gentiles lord it over them, and their high officials exercise authority over them. Not so with you. Instead, whoever wants to become great among you must be your servant, and whoever wants to be first must be slave of all. For even the Son of Man did not come to be served, but to serve, and to give his life as a ransom for many."

In today's world there is a general feeling that those who are well-educated are not expected to serve but to lead—as if those concepts are mutually exclusive. John 13 tells us that they are not. What an intriguing and overpowering manifestation of servant leadership it was—Christ, Himself, willing to do whatever needed to be done! And yet, when I read this passage, there is no doubt in my mind as to Who was the leader in that upper room. While girding Himself and kneeling to wash his disciples' feet, He remained in total command of the situation. The Servant was the Leader.

Having been elected as a leader in the church, I cannot read John 13 often enough! And each time I kneel down to wash someone's feet, I hear the echo of a very pertinent question: You may want to be a leader, but how about your willingness to be a servant?

16 Spiritual Gifts and Ministries

God bestows upon all members of His church in every age spiritual gifts which each member is to employ in loving ministry for the common good of the church and of humanity. Given by the agency of the  *Holy Spirit, who apportions to each member as He wills, the gifts provide all abilities and ministries needed by the church to fulfill its divinely ordained functions. According to the Scriptures, these gifts include such ministries as faith, healing, prophecy, proclamation, teaching, administration, reconciliation, compassion, and self-sacrificing service and charity for the help and encouragement of people. Some members are called of God and are endowed by the Spirit for functions recognized by the church in pastoral, evangelistic, apostolic, and teaching ministries, particularly needed to equip the members for service, to build up the church to spiritual maturity, and to foster unity of the faith and knowledge of God. When members employ these spiritual gifts as faithful stewards of God's varied grace, the church is protected from the destructive influence of false doctrine, grows with a growth that is from God, and is built up in faith and love.*

Rom. 12:4-8; 1 Cor. 12:9-11, 27, 28; Eph. 4:8, 11-16; Acts 6:1-7; 1 Tim. 3:1-13; 1 Peter 4:10, 11.

Chapter 16

Inspiration

As members of the Seventh-day Adventist Church we are constantly bombarded with appeals to take part in all kinds of activities. Not only are there almost as many "offices" in the church (elders, deacons, Sabbath School teachers, youth sponsors, Pathfinder leaders, etc., etc.) that need to be filled as there are members in an average congregation, but there is also a multitude of programs for which volunteers are needed.

The tragedy is that some aspire to positions for which they are totally unsuited, while others with very clear skills and abilities are extremely reluctant to offer their services. Many of those in the latter category are so busy in their everyday life that they carefully protect the little spare time they have and shy away from extra burdens and responsibilities.

The doctrine of stewardship and the doctrine of spiritual gifts are closely linked yet must not be confused with each other. We all have natural abilities, acquired skills, special talents, and a unique life- and work-experience. The doctrine of stewardship tells us that we must utilize these skills and abilities. Some of us are more richly endowed with natural abilities than others. Some of us have a wider experience and have more technical know-how in certain areas of life than others. But all of us have some talent or talents and all of these ought to be put to optimal use, in the context of our home, our work, the society of which we are part, and our church! When selecting people for specific assignments or asking people to volunteer for specific tasks, we would be foolish not to make an earnest effort to match the requirements for these jobs with the abilities of individuals.

The doctrine of spiritual gifts, however, adds an extra dimension to this. God knows our limitations, and He has therefore graciously made provision to enhance our natural abilities and skills or to go even further: to equip us with knowledge, skills, abilities, and insights that we did not acquire through our education, background, or experience. He does this with one single purpose in mind: that we may be able to serve His church in a much more efficient and powerful way.

The various passages of Scripture that list these spiritual gifts are not identical, although they overlap a fair deal. The lists are probably not meant to be exhaustive, but they do make clear that the gifts take on many forms, varying from the rather mundane gifts of helping and leading to the more spectacular gifts such as prophecy, speaking in tongues, and healing. The gifts have a clear purpose: They are given to strengthen and nurture the church. One other point is significant: The Holy Spirit determines how they are distributed and who receives how much of which gift.

It would seem logical that we first of all try to find out what gift(s) we might have and that we then attempt to find a niche in the church where we can use not only our acquired skills and life-experience but, in particular, the spiritual gift that we have been given. And it would also seem logical that we stay away from assignments that are not in line with our natural abilities and our spiritual gift(s).

This, I think, leads to the logical conclusion that we do not have to respond positively to every appeal or accept any assignment the church tries to unload on us. If the church fails to discern our talents and gifts, it is up to us to make sure that we do not do what others can do better and leave our own talents and gifts unused.

Give your best

In the country where I grew up and spent the first fifteen or so years of my ministry, door-to-door work (for Harvest Ingathering and for other purposes) was one of the few methods of witnessing that were practiced. I was never very good in selling magazines from door to door. When I went, it was with lead in my shoes. In retrospect, I should have looked more intently for a niche in the activities of the church that better fitted my talents and spiritual gifts.

Today I feel considerably more relaxed about my contribution to church life. I know there are quite a few gifts I do not have. But I also realize I have certain skills and certain abilities. I have acquired, for instance, considerable communication skills. I do not count myself among the great authors of our time, but I do find it relatively easy to put ideas on paper. I have improved those skills through conscious efforts and years of practice. When I sit behind my keyboard and give the creative juices free reign, I find that often things flow much easier than I anticipated, and I find words and phrases that later astound me. Call it "inspiration" if you want. Whatever it is, I believe I may safely call it my spiritual gift.

Does God expect me to do all kinds of things for which I have little ability and which require gifts that He has not given me? I believe He does not. I may feel perfectly free to say No to those things that I am not equipped to do, since I miss both the relevant experience and the necessary "gift." I know that my niche is not in Pathfinder work nor in organizing a social evening. I do not think it is my forte to hold evangelistic campaigns or to do pastoral work for elderly people. I can serve the church in other ways. Writing is one of them. If there is anything of value in what I write, it is partly the fruit of experience and long practice but not in the least also the result of exercising my spiritual gift. Therefore, do not blame me for being a bit reluctant when it comes to Harvest Ingathering or work on the social committee. I have stopped blaming myself for my lack of enthusiasm for these and similar activities. I no longer feel guilty when I say No to being involved in certain programs. I do not need to feel guilty as long as I say wholeheartedly Yes to those activities for which I possess some talents and for which I have been equipped by the Spirit.

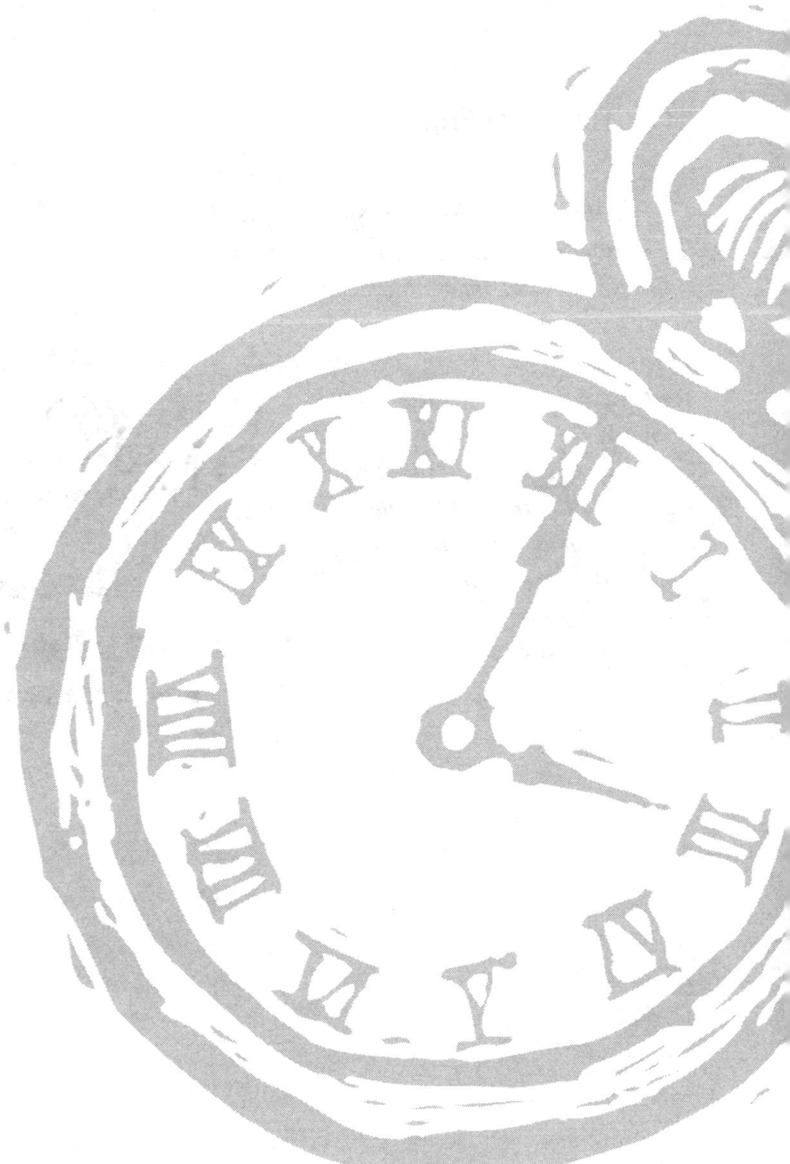

17 The Gift of Prophecy

One of the gifts of the Holy Spirit is prophecy. This gift is an identifying mark of the remnant church and was manifested in the ministry of Ellen G. White. As the Lord's messenger, her writings are a continuing and authoritative source of truth which provide for the church comfort, guidance, instruction, and correction. They also make clear that the Bible is the standard by which all teaching and experience must be tested.

**Joel 2:28, 29;
Acts 2:14-21; Heb. 1:1-3;
Rev. 12:17; 19:10.**

Chapter 17

Ellen G. White and My Denominational Career

Some chapters in this book are more difficult to write than others. I hope it has become clear that I try to be honest and intend to stay away from mere pious clichés. And that is also my intention as I write the next few pages. I am acutely aware that some may begin the reading of this book with this very chapter, to see whether the author is "kosher" when it comes to the "Spirit of Prophecy." After all, he is a European, and the rumor seems to have spread to other parts of the world that European Adventists are a bit "easy" when it comes to Mrs. White!

Well, let me begin by devoting a few lines to this myth that European Adventists pay less attention to the writings of Ellen G. White than American Adventists. I think that, having lived and worked on both sides of the Atlantic, I have a fair idea of what the score is. There is no evidence whatsoever that European Adventists in general are "softer" on the Spirit of Prophecy than North American Adventists. There may be a tendency to be somewhat selective in applying Ellen White's counsels, but I have noticed that tendency on both sides of the great pond. European Adventists in general may just be a bit more candid in admitting where they take the liberty to deviate from such counsel than their American sisters and brethren are.

There is no doubt that the Seventh-day Adventist Church and Ellen G. White are inseparably linked. It is impossible to be an Adventist without recognizing her vital role in Adventism. But having said that, I hasten to add that there seems to be an awful lot of misunderstanding about that role. Let me mention two problem areas.

First, although all Adventists would agree that the Bible is the ultimate standard for our faith and practice, many adhere to that principle only in theory, while in actual practice they elevate Mrs. White above the Bible and give her the last word in every detail of doctrine, Bible exegesis, and lifestyle.

Second, many do not sufficiently realize that, if we believe Ellen White's writings to be divinely inspired, we must have just as solid a hermeneutic (system of interpretation) when dealing with her writings as we need when studying the Scriptures. We can only hope to learn the right lessons from the Bible when we ask the right questions and carefully distinguish eternal truth from the cultural wrappings of the places where the various parts of the Bible were written and of the time when they were first committed to parchment. We recognize that society in the time of King Saul, or in the earliest churches in Asia Minor, was significantly different from our Western twentieth century world and take that into account as we read the Bible. But the America of a century ago also vastly differed from our modern setting. In fact, the situation in the New World went through a number of distinct stages during Ellen White's lifetime, and she showed herself to be much more flexible and adaptable to changing circumstances than many of her devoted readers today seem to be.

I feel that the church could and should have done more in helping the members to have a more balanced view of the prophet. She must certainly not be ignored. But neither must she be placed on such a pedestal that she becomes more than she ever claimed to be and wanted to be. (George R. Knight's recent book *Meet Ellen White—A fresh look at her life, writings, and major themes*, published by the Review and Herald in 1996, is an example of the kind of material that is needed!)

I also happen to feel that the sheer endless production of compilations has often done more harm than good. And—dare I say it?—I sense that at times an almost magical power is attributed to some of her books. When I worked as an editorial consultant on the African continent, I was repeatedly confronted with the idea that publishing books like *The Great Controversy* would be a panacea for all the ills, not only of the publishing work, but also for the church as a whole in Africa. But the undeniable fact is that in many areas the people do not have the basic knowledge, either of the Bible or of history, to read such a book with profit. Just recently I met the same phenomenon in Albania, a tiny country with about three million inhabitants. After a period of several decades of militant atheism, most people are biblically illiterate. The Adventist Church has once again established a presence, but it is still extremely weak: just a few hundred members with at best some basic knowledge of the message of the Bible. There is virtually no Adventist literature in the Albanian language, not even a small paperback publication that, in simple language, explains the main tenets of the Christian faith! Yet, a translation of *The Great Controversy* has been produced, and some believers have become convinced that publishing this particular book is the highest priority. I feel quite strongly that my belief in the prophetic gift of Ellen G. White does not require me to support such premature projects.

But having said these things, I do not want to leave any doubt about my profound conviction that God has blessed His church by providing a source of prophetic counsel. It has given the church direction and has been a (or rather: the) major factor in making the church what it is today. Those who know the basics of Adventist history will remember how Ellen White repeatedly steered the Adventist community away from extremism and fanaticism and how she emphasized a Christ-centered message over and against the legalistic views of many of her contemporaries. I thank God that the greatest author of the Adventist Church is not Uriah Smith but Ellen G. White!

One of the most significant contributions Ellen White made to Adventism was her development of the great controversy theme. We must recognize that lots of things have changed in the world and that her actual presentation of that theme may need some updating, since the world in which present-day Adventists live is no longer characterized by a predominantly North American religious scene with only Protestants and Roman Catholics! But her underlying philosophy of history is a concept that has greatly helped me, as it has helped millions of others, to make more sense out of what is happening around us.

One of the things I find so attractive in the teaching of my church is that it offers a holistic message; it addresses humankind as integrated beings of body, mind and spirit. In recent years this view of humans has gained ground around us, but it has always been a vital element of Adventist beliefs. Those who know something of the history of our denomination remember that we owe this facet of our faith foremost to Ellen White.

My own career in the church would have been very different had there been no Ellen White. I have spent more than twenty years in Adventist education and in the publishing system of the church. Would the school of which I was a principal have been established if there had been no prophetic voice that called for an educational system? And would there have been publishing houses in Europe and in Africa, where I served with so much satisfaction, had there not been the prophetic prompting to start printing and publishing?

I rather doubt it. So I may sometimes wonder how some of her counsels ought to be applied today, but there is no doubt in my mind that Ellen White has affected the corporate church as well as my own personal life in a most profound way.

18 The Law of God

The great principles of God's law are embodied in the Ten Commandments and exemplified in the life of Christ. They express God's love, will, and purposes concerning human conduct and relationships and are binding upon all people in every age. These precepts are the basis of God's covenant with His people and the standard in God's judgment. Through the agency of the Holy Spirit they point out sin and awaken a sense of need for a Saviour. Salvation is all of grace and not of works, but its fruitage is obedience to the Commandments. This obedience develops Christian character and results in a sense of well-being. It is an evidence of our love for the Lord and our concern for our fellow men. The obedience of faith demonstrates the power of Christ to transform lives, and therefore strengthens Christian witness.

Exod. 20:1-17; Ps. 40:7, 8;

Matt. 22:36-40;

Deut. 28:1-14; Matt. 5:17-20;

Heb. 8:8-10; John 15:7-10;

Eph. 2:8-10; 1 John 5:3;

Rom. 8:3, 4; Ps. 19:7-14.

Chapter 18

No Sailing Under False Colors

Adventists have been accused of being legalists: They emphasize obedience to the law rather than the grace of Christ. Unfortunately, there has often been more truth in that criticism than we are willing to admit. There are some mitigating circumstances, however. I believe it would be true to say that many of the denominations in the nineteenth-century world, in which Adventism originated, focused more intensely on rules and outward conduct than they do today. And it is certainly true that Adventists were often forced by their opponents to explain why they insisted keeping all Ten Commandments—the Sabbath included. This inevitably made it appear that Adventists majored heavily in the law and in obedience to the law as a prerequisite for acceptance by God.

But we must admit that many Adventists not only appeared to be somewhat legalistic, since they were time and again required to defend their Sabbath keeping and their belief that the divine law had not been abrogated at the Cross, but continued to be valid— they in fact were very often extremely legalistic. The most important and bitterest theological conflict in the church was precisely over this issue. The debates of the 1888 General Conference in Minneapolis about Righteousness by Faith reverberated for many decades. And there are still some today who rather vocally proclaim that the church has not adequately learned its lessons on that point and has rejected rather than embraced the truth of righteousness by faith.

The ongoing discussion about what exactly happened in Minneapolis and how many supported and resisted the "new theology" in the aftermath of 1888 is interesting but largely academic. There is no doubt today where Adventism officially stands. It firmly sides with those who believe that we are saved by grace and that obedience to God's law is the fruit of that grace; it is the result of being saved and not the basis upon which salvation is given as a reward! The trouble today is not with official Adventist teaching; it is with countless individuals who still live in a very legalistic way in spite of their insistence that they believe wholeheartedly in righteousness by faith. This is a serious matter. For the people involved, since they are in great spiritual danger as their focus shifts from what Christ does for them to what they themselves do for Christ. It is impossible to say how many people have left the church or how many people have decided not to join the church because of the presence of this legalistic attitude!

The covenant

When I think about the law of God, and in particular about its expression in the Ten Commandments, two elements stand out in my mind in a special way.

Many years ago, when I worked for my master's degree at the Seventh-day Adventist Theological Seminary at Andrews University, Dr. Siegfried Horn, the renowned Old Testament scholar and archeologist, during one of his classes in "Old Testament Backgrounds," explained how the form in which the Bible has transmitted the Ten Commandments is extremely significant. The content of the Ten Commandments was, of course, eternal—the principles of the law were revealed long before Moses went up the mountain to receive the two tablets of stone. But when God decided to reiterate the eternal principles of his law, he used a form that was known to the people in Moses' day. The Hittite rulers made covenants with the peoples they subdued, and the terms of the covenant always consisted of a historical prologue followed by a number of rules to govern the relationship of the subdued peoples to the Hittite ruler and a number of stipulations to govern the relationships between the various peoples that were under the Hittite rule. Such a treaty had a significant implication. It was a covenant: The subdued nations had the absolute guarantee of protection by the mighty Hittite ruler as long as they followed the stipulations of the treaty. Knowing this historical background was nothing less than a revelation for me. That, apparently, was what God wanted to make clear through the form in which He now revealed His will: I guarantee complete and absolute protection as long as you, My people, follow some simple rules!

That is still, I believe, a lesson we need to learn. Of course, there will be punishment for those who willfully disregard God's law. But the emphasis is not on the threat, on what will happen if we turn our backs on God. The emphasis is on what God wants to do for us: He wants to be our Protector; He wants to see us through, whatever happens. A few simple rules help us to stay on the right track. They help us to be His people so that He can remain our God.

There is another aspect to this: If God was so meticulous in choosing a form that was relevant to those who were living in Moses' day, should that not urge us also to search for relevant forms and expressions, as we try to retell the gospel story to our contemporaries? Should the supreme example of contextualization in the Ten Commandments not motivate us also to contextualize our message in such a way that it catches the attention of the people in the diverse cultures in which the message must be preached? I firmly believe we should never compromise the content of our message, but we have the duty to find forms that are relevant to the people we seek to reach. In some way I owe that conviction to a large extent to the train of thought that was set in motion in Berrien Springs in the winter of 1965/66.

Making it fit today

Considering the New Testament reminder (in the Sermon on the Mount, for example) that we ought to pursue the spirit of the Ten Commandments rather than merely the letter, these ten principles pose lifelong challenges. Not to murder in the literal sense of the word is well within the boundaries of what most of us can achieve. Not to hate, or to thoroughly dislike some people is, however, a more difficult task. Not to cheat on your spouse by secretly meeting someone may not be too hard, but to fully honor the spirit of the seventh commandment is for many of us a different matter. Shopping on Sabbath is not a real temptation (at least not for me), but truly celebrating the Lord's day in a meaningful way is the project of a lifetime.

For me personally the third commandment seems to offer the greatest challenge: "You shall not misuse the name of God, for the Lord will not hold anyone guiltless, who misuses His name." Swearing and abusive language are not the only things this commandment condemns. Years ago I read a book on the Ten Commandments. I do not recollect the name of the author or the title, but I do remember that I was struck by the writer's comments on the third commandment. He said: This commandment tells us that we should not sail under false colors. We cannot use the name of the Lord just as a pretext. We cannot link His name to activities He does not approve of or as a pious dressing that covers our own hobby horses.

Recentl, an independent Adventist publication printed an article in which the writer testified how God had blessed her. She had been impressed that she ought to keep the Sabbath more faithfully and ought not to take a shower on Sabbath morning. But that posed a tremendous problem: How would she get through the Sabbath day with greasy hair? So she made a deal with the Lord: If I will no longer take my shower on Sabbath morning, will You then please take care of my greasy hair?"

Reading that I thought: This is a sad example of taking the name of the Lord in vain! This is linking the name of the Lord to the kind of legalistic reasoning that He abhors.

But recognizing this transgression of the third commandment in what others say and do does not help me very much in my personal challenge. How many times have I asked the Lord's blessing for the day ahead of me and have then proceeded with my program in ways that He certainly would not approve of? I realize beginning the day with invoking His name and then proceeding on my own steam is like pouring a pious dressing over my schedule and is, in fact, abuse of His holy name. How many times have I chaired or attended a meeting that began with a prayer: "Please, God, be present with your Spirit. Guide us in our discussions and decisions"— but five minutes later unproven accusations, half-truths, and other un-Christian remarks would fly across the table? When that happens, God's name has been seriously abused.

As I contemplate God's law, I sense that I need His transforming grace if I am ever going to live up to the spirit of His golden rules! I must make it my objective to live so that everything I do and say is a truthful affirmation of His holy name.

19 The Sabbath

The beneficent Creator, after the six days of Creation, rested on the seventh day and instituted the Sabbath for all people as a memorial of Creation. The fourth commandment of God's unchange-able law requires the observance of this seventh-day Sabbath as the day of rest, worship, and ministry in harmony with the teachings and practice of Jesus, the Lord of the Sabbath. The Sabbath is a day of delightful commu-nion with God and one another. It is a symbol of our redemption in Christ, a sign of our sanctification, a token of our allegiance, and a fore-taste of our eternal future in God's kingdom. The Sabbath is God's perpetual sign of His eter-nal covenant between Him and His people. Joyful observance of this holy time from evening to evening, sunset to sunset, is a celebration of God's creative and redemptive acts.

Gen. 2:1-3; Exod. 20:8-11;

Luke 4:16; Isa. 56:5, 6;

58:13,14; Matt. 12:1-12;

Exod. 31:13-17;

Ezek. 20:12, 20;

Deut. 5:12-15; Heb. 4:1-11;

Lev. 23:32; Mark 1:32.

Chapter 19

The Real Thing

For a long time I kept Sunday on Sabbath. I grew up in a small village twenty-five miles north of Amsterdam, the Netherlands. The village population could be divided roughly into three groups: one-third Roman Catholic; one-third (rather liberal) Dutch Reformed; and one-third (rather conservative) Christian Reformed. Each group had its own church and its own primary school. Although there was no open hostility between the three groups, there was not much social contact, either, in particular, between the two Protestant groups and the Catholics. There were just two anomalies: one Jehovah's Witness family and one Seventh-day Adventist family.

Ours was a truly unique situation. My grandfather, who lived with us, was an active member of the Dutch Reformed Church. He derived considerable status from the fact that he was a close friend of the minister of the village church. With my older sister I attended the Dutch Reformed Sunday school for some time. Nobody seemed to find that strange, and never was there, as far as I can remember, any suggestion that this might be an attempt to wean us away from Adventism. My sisters and I attended the Christian Reformed elementary school. Considering the three options, this seemed the best alternative for us as Adventist children. The

Christian Reformed at the time were very conservative in their theology and were strict Sunday keepers. I think that in the eyes of most of the villagers we were very much like the Christian Reformed, except that Saturday was for some strange reason our Sunday.

Sunday keeping was a serious matter for the Christian Reformed people in our village. Most would go to church twice—for the (very long) morning service and the (long) afternoon service. Most adhered to the strict code of dos and don'ts. No extensive travel, no shopping, no sports, no visits to either of the two village pubs, no bicycle riding. Church attendance, a good meal, some social visiting, and—weather permitting—a walk.

To me, as a child, Sabbath keeping was much like that. Riding a bike on Sabbath was no issue, for my parents could not afford to give me one until I was about twelve. Playing sports never was an issue, either, for I did not like sports. But for the rest, Sabbath was Sunday on Saturday. Except of course for the fact that our Sabbath began on Friday evening and ended on Saturday evening. In the winter the Sabbath would end as early as 4:00 p.m. As soon as the sun had set, my mother would often send me to the bakery to get fresh bread. In the summer the bakery would keep some bread for us, and even after the shop had closed we could knock on the back door and get our bread. In retrospect, I wonder what the owner of the bakery shop made of that aspect of our religion. Our Sabbath surely made us different from the rest of the village!

Sabbath keeping had its challenges during my years in secondary school. I had to miss classes on Saturday morning, and although the school administration and the teachers were quite helpful, my Sabbath keeping did give me a status aparte in the class, which I did not relish.

Going on to an Adventist college, first in the Netherlands and subsequently in England, meant a dramatic change. No longer was there a social stigma attached to Sabbath observance, but there was another problem. Often the Sabbath was the most boring day of the week! In that respect there seems to have been but little change over the years, for my son reported the very same sentiments when, a few decades later, he attended two different Adventist colleges in the United States.

What to do

The question of what to do and what not to do on Sabbath kept coming back as I began to work for the church and, even stronger, as I began to travel. I found that the set of rules, as to what is permitted on Sabbath and what is not, differs from place to place. Dutch Adventists would not dream of going to a museum on the Sabbath. But when I attended a youth rally in Belgium for the first time, I found that our more conservative Southern neighbors had a special treat for the participants on the Sabbath afternoon: a visit to a museum! In a Dutch Adventist youth camp playing a friendly game of soccer on the Sabbath afternoon raised no eyebrows, but I later learned that this never failed to elicit strong criticism from visiting Adventist dignitaries. When I began to move around in the world, this picture of different "boundaries" for the Sabbath was confirmed time and again. Who can, for instance, deny that, in general, Sabbath keeping in the Eastern United States has a different dimension from that in the West?

To some people this feature of our church life is distinctly worrying: How can people with the same Bible and the same fundamental beliefs be so different in their Sabbath worship? My reaction is rather the opposite: I have found it very liberating to discover that true Sabbath keeping does not depend on a precise set of dos and don'ts. The way in which we keep the Sabbath is in many ways culturally determined. We will (and should) all create certain boundaries to separate what we normally do on the other six days from what we do on God's special day, the Sabbath. But "the real thing," the essence of the Sabbath, is not in what I do or abstain from doing. Rather, it is found in what, in some mysterious way, God does for me. Certainly, I am well advised to create a setting that helps me to experience God's blessing. It is much easier to experience a sense of awe in a majestic cathedral than it is in a disco or a casino or in a busy airport or in the London "tube." Likewise, it is much easier to sense God's presence and His special Sabbath blessing if we erect certain boundaries around that day to ensure that there is space for God to maneuver in.

The real thing

I just referred to the Sabbath as "the real thing." That is what we as Adventists believe. Sunday worship no doubt is very meaningful to many Christians and, on the other hand, Sabbath keeping is little more than a shallow tradition for many Adventists. But viewed from the biblical perspective, Sabbath keeping is "the real thing." And through the years my relationship to the Sabbath has more and more shifted from a predominantly rational, doctrinal conviction to an experiential truth: Here is "the real thing," made from a unique (divine) recipe.

Comparing the Sabbath to Coca-Cola (advertised as "the real thing" among all refreshments) is apt in yet another way. Although Coca-Cola cannot boast the same long history as Sabbath keeping, it has probably established a presence in about as many countries as the Sabbath has. Admittedly, Sabbath keepers are a usually small minority, but they can be found, whether you are on the southern tip of South America or above the Arctic Circle in northern Norway; whether you are in Los Angeles or Seoul, in a village near Lake Titicaca or near Lake Victoria. Wherever you go, you can find "the real thing." It is nothing short of a divine miracle that this unique institution has survived through the ages and is today appreciated by millions of people all over the world.

Accepting God's gift of the Sabbath adds a dimension to life that I would not want to be without. Yes, it makes me different: I stand out from the crowd. But it also makes me different through the divine peace it imports into my busy life and in providing me with that unique time slot that I need to work on my relationship with God, my family, and with God's creation. I, for one, feel "special" that I can play a small part in helping to extend the unique blessing of the Sabbath both horizontally and vertically: to help spread the message as widely as possible that this divine blessing is available and to challenge my fellow believers to experience "the real thing" in a more profound way.

20 Stewardship

We are God's stewards, entrusted by Him with time and opportunities, abilities and possessions, and the blessings of the earth and its resources. We are responsible to Him for their proper use. We acknowledge God's ownership by faithful service to Him and our fellow men, and by returning tithes and giving offerings for the proclamation of His gospel and the support and growth of His church. Stewardship is a privilege given to us by God for nurture in love and the victory over selfishness and covetousness. The steward rejoices in the blessings that come to others as a result of his faithfulness.

Gen. 1:26-28; 2:15;

1 Chron. 29:14; Hag. 1:3-11;

Mal. 3:8-12; 1 Cor. 9:9-14;

Matt. 23:23; 2 Cor. 8:1-15;

Rom. 15:26, 27.

Chapter 20

**First
Things
First**

In many places in the world the church is in financial difficulties. In some of the economically challenged areas of the globe the church is a victim of its own success. The problem is that "the work" is not self-supporting; that is, new congregations do not contribute enough to pay for their own pastor, and growing institutions need more and more subsidy. It is tragic but true: In some countries we really cannot afford to win too many people. Because, the larger the church becomes, the more difficult it becomes to meet its financial needs!

Pakistan is one such place. I have a special interest in Pakistan. The Trans-European Division has been entrusted with the care for that predominantly Muslim country. As one of the leaders of the division, I have been part of many discussions how to deal with the challenges of bringing the gospel to Pakistan. It is, of course, almost impossible (and even dangerous) to reach the Muslim population. But there are a few million non-Muslims who are "reachable." They are mostly among the poorest of the poor and live in ghettos in towns or in "Christian" villages. We could probably win tens of thousands of these people if we just had the resources. There is little problem in finding a foreign evangelist who is willing to go for four or five weeks for an evangelistic campaign. He may baptize a hundred or more people. But then there must be a modest building to house the new congregation; there must be a small school to provide education for the children and literacy classes for the adults; there must be a pastor/teacher who will nurture the group of new believers. The sad truth is we do not have the funds to do this on any significant scale, and thus the opportunities remain largely unused.

Albania is another example of the same tragic reality. After decades of atheistic dictatorship, it is now possible to preach the gospel with a fair amount of freedom. The Adventist Church has reestablished its presence. As I write, we have about two hundred baptized believers; there are two missionaries and two or three young Albanian trainees to look after the needs of these members and to further develop the church, besides an ADRA office that struggles to stay solvent. So many opportunities, so many needs, and yet so little we can do because the resources are not there.

In many of the Western European countries the circumstances are quite different, but there is an equally pressing financial problem. As long as the church was growing, all was relatively well. But in most of Western Europe a new paganism has eroded much of traditional Christianity. The churches are fighting for survival and the Seventh-day Adventist Church is not immune to this general decline in Christianity. And thus a vicious circle begins: Because there is no growth in membership, there is no growth in income. Somehow, expenses always seem to go up, and thus the number of pastors must be cut, and no funds are left for new, imaginative methods of evangelism!

We would be a different church if all members paid a faithful tithe and if all members systematically supported their local church, the projects in their country, and foreign missions in a substantial way. Exact statistics about the percentage of our church members who give "a faithful tithe" are hard to come by, but in many places this has dropped well below the 50 percent mark. Just imagine if that percentage would increase to 75 or 80 percent. And what if all offerings would increase in the same way? We would have a different church. So many things would be possible. So many initiatives could get off the ground, and so many opportunities and challenges could be met.

Now, I know that I have seldom faced the same problems that most church members face. Ever since I have been a church employee (with the exception of a few years in the United States), my tithes have been deducted from my salary. Thus the temptation to use some of that money for myself has been sharply reduced. I realize that for many it takes real courage and means real sacrifice to give 10 percent or more to the church. And I sympathize with those who have not always been able to practice this "fundamental belief" of supporting God's work in the biblical way. But things could become dramatically better for the church if a larger percentage of church members lived up to this basic principle of Christian stewardship.

Unfortunately, the church has often failed to teach adequately the principles of true stewardship to converts in developing countries. This is wrong, because it robs the believers of an important aspect of Christian experience, and it impedes the church in its growth and development. Some might say, Well it does not make all that much difference. Our members in Africa are poor, so their tithe and offerings do not amount to much anyway. That is not true; however, if a few million people would be truly faithful in being stewards over the little they have, this would bring a very significant income into the church's "storehouse." And, staying closer to home, I know that various factors have had an adverse effect on giving patterns in the Western world. They need to be addressed. The church cannot prosper if it does not have the means to function properly. And we cannot prosper spiritually if we remain so much attached to our material possessions that we refuse to give God His part.

Not just money

Although I recognize that at times I also could be more generous when the needs of the church are presented and I hear an urgent appeal to help, I must confess that my main deficiency in the area of stewardship does not have to do with money but rather with time.

I did learn a few things during the years I worked in Africa. One of them was that it is possible to gain a healthy attitude toward time by striving to find a midpoint between the frustrating disregard for time so often manifested by people on the African continent and the Western obsession with time, where every minute counts and timetables and deadlines are objects of worship.

But still, being a good and faithful steward of my time remains a tall order.

Often I find that the famous Twenty-Eighty Law of Pareto is operative in my life. According to this law we have a tendency to spend 80 percent of our time on routine matters—things that possibly we should not even deal with ourselves, or we should quickly dispose of so that most of our time is invested in things that really count. However, in reality, only a small portion of our time gets used for the truly important things. This, naturally, leads to frustration. And believe me, I know what I am talking about: working (too) many hours and still being left with the feeling that you have not done anything!

Christian stewardship has just as much to do with time as with money. Time is a precious commodity. We have only a limited quantity. We cannot afford to waste it. But neither can we afford to spend all of it behind our desks or in other work situations. We must somehow plan our schedule to allow time for family, for church activities (the order is deliberate), and for recreation. But also for our spiritual life, for self-development, and study. I must confess that in this area I have a long way to go. I have taught classes on time management. I know the theory, but I fall terribly short when it comes to practicing those principles. So while many of my fellow church members ought to get their act together in the financial aspects of stewardship, I also have my challenge cut out for me.

21 Christian Behavior

We are called to be a godly people who think, feel, and act in harmony with the principles of heaven. For the Spirit to recreate in us the character of our Lord we involve ourselves only in those things that will produce Christlike purity, health, and joy in our lives. This means that our amusement and entertainment should meet the highest standards of Christian taste and beauty. While recognizing cultural differences, our dress is to be simple, modest, and neat, befitting those whose true beauty does not consist in outward adornment but in the imperishable ornament of a gentle and quiet spirit. It also means that because our bodies are the temples of the Holy Spirit, we are to care for them intelligently. Along with adequate exercise and rest, we are to adopt the most healthful diet possible and abstain from the unclean foods identified in the Scriptures. Since alcoholic beverages, tobacco, and the irresponsible use of drugs and narcotics are harmful to our bodies, we are to abstain from them as well. Instead, we are to engage in whatever brings our thoughts and bodies into the discipline of Christ, who desires our wholesomeness, joy, and goodness.

Rom. 12:1, 2; 1 John 2:6;

Eph. 5:1-21; Phil. 4:8;

2 Cor. 10:5; 6:14-7:1;

1 Peter 3:1-4;

1 Cor. 6:19, 20; 10:31;

Lev. 11:1-47; 3 John 2.

Chapter 21

Living XL

The Adventist lifestyle—peace and reconciliation rather than war and controversy, happy families rather than broken homes, temperance rather than addiction, healthful living rather than junk food, clean fun rather than a film/TV-video overdose of sex and violence. Does it exist? Or is it a figment of the imagination? Is "the Adventist lifestyle" something that only exists in Adventist literature, or is it a reality in Adventist lives?

There is no doubt that on the average Adventists live healthier and longer than the population at large. Research in a number of countries—the United States, Australia, Norway, the Netherlands, New Zealand, Poland, and elsewhere—has conclusively shown that Adventists have a higher than average life expectancy and are less likely to die of certain serious illnesses. Less meat consumption, far less smoking, and far less alcohol consumption are invariably singled out as the key factors. (We would be kidding others and ourselves if we said that most Adventists are vegetarians and that all Adventists have totally rejected the use of tobacco and alcohol.)

Vegetarianism is the preferred option for the Seventh-day Adventist diet. From my European perspective this does not seem such an important issue as it is in the American context where meat is a much larger component of the normal daily food intake. Let me

125

just say in passing that I applaud those vegetarians who are consistent, without making their diet the all-important aspect of their religion and considering themselves part of a spiritual elite. And let me add that I have often been amazed how easily many vegetarians (even church leaders) can be persuaded that while traveling "it is impossible to be vegetarian!" I fear that if the full truth were known, we would find quite a difference between what many eat and drink in the privacy of their homes or in places where they are anonymous and what they consume when other Adventist eyes are watching them. I know I am far from perfect, but I have tried to be honest and not to display a public image that does not match what I do when I am at home.

I must say that I continue to be happy about the position my church takes with regard to alcohol, tobacco, and other drugs. Whether or not it can conclusively be proven from the Bible that drinking an occasional glass of wine is a sin, I am thankful for the traditional position of the church with regard to smoking and drinking. And even if the theological arguments were not as strong as some may want them to be, what reason could there be to change our position, considering the incalculable misery caused by the suffering and premature deaths resulting from tobacco addiction? And what reason could there be for relaxing our stand on alcohol in view of the immeasurable misery alcohol produces?

I owe it to my Adventist upbringing that alcohol and tobacco have never become part of my life and that I am so ignorant on the subject of other drugs that I would not recognize cocaine or even marijuana if I saw these substances. Sure, I have had my teenage experiments with cigarettes and have had a few beers. I have tasted wine and even once smoked a cigar! But the Adventist standpoint regarding these addictive habits have, I am convinced, prevented me from making them part of my lifestyle. I am sure my children have also had their experiments; they may have experimented a bit more than I did in my youth. But the fact that we have never had an addiction problem in our home and that they, as far as I know (and I am pretty certain about this), have upon leaving their parental home stayed away from hard and soft drugs and do not smoke, is probably to be credited to the Adventist environment during their formative years. So if there is one "fundamental belief" that definitely had a positive impact on my life, it is this one.

I have to confess that, like most Adventists, I am somewhat selective in the elements of the Adventist lifestyle that I practice. I may do well when it comes to refraining from unclean food and abstaining from tobacco and alcohol, but I do quite poorly in the area of rest and physical exercise. In spite of all New Year's resolutions, I remain a workaholic and keep postponing a serious exercise plan, while trying to convince myself that my waistline is only extending at a very slow pace! This very fact, however, should remind me not to be too judgmental when others fail to comply with some aspects of the Adventist lifestyle that I have no problem with.

Total lifestyle

This "fundamental belief" covers a lot of ground. It also deals with modesty in the way we dress and has a bearing on the famous issue of jewelry. Enough has been said and is being said about this particular issue. Unfortunately this subject has often given rise to an unhealthy, petty, legalistic bickering, without due attention to the underlying broad principles and cultural differences.

Another area this "fundamental belief" touches upon is that of our recreation and the way we spend our leisure time. We are told that these ought to synchronize with the highest norms of Christian taste and beauty. Here, once again, is a very concrete issue where I can testify that Christianity (yes, Adventism, if you please) has made a difference in my life. Over the years I have become much more selective in how I spend my free time, in particular, in what I see and read. When I want to unwind, watching television is still my preferred option. But I have become much more selective in what I watch. And that is not just because my satellite dish has given me over fifty channels to "surf." The same goes for reading. I am a voracious reader, always reading several books at the same time—usually a mixture of heavy and lighter material. But here again, I have become considerably more selective and not because I can now afford to buy more books than in the past. Analyzing this tendency toward greater selectivity, I must conclude that this is not so much a conscious effort of my will. I do not have to force myself not to see certain films or not to read certain books. Quite a few things simply no longer interest me in the way they did thirty, twenty, or even ten years ago. I do not want to waste my time on them. There are so many other more worthwhile things to do, see, and read.

There is no doubt that practicing this particular fundamental belief, which impacts so intensely on our lifestyle, greatly improves the quality of life. This statement is not just a matter of theology and morality—although it is that also. But it enables us in a tangible and measurable way to enjoy life more fully, more deeply—and, most likely, quite a bit longer. I am happy for the advances I have made in applying the principles of this fundamental belief in my life. And I thank God that here at least is an area where I have clearly experienced some spiritual growth!

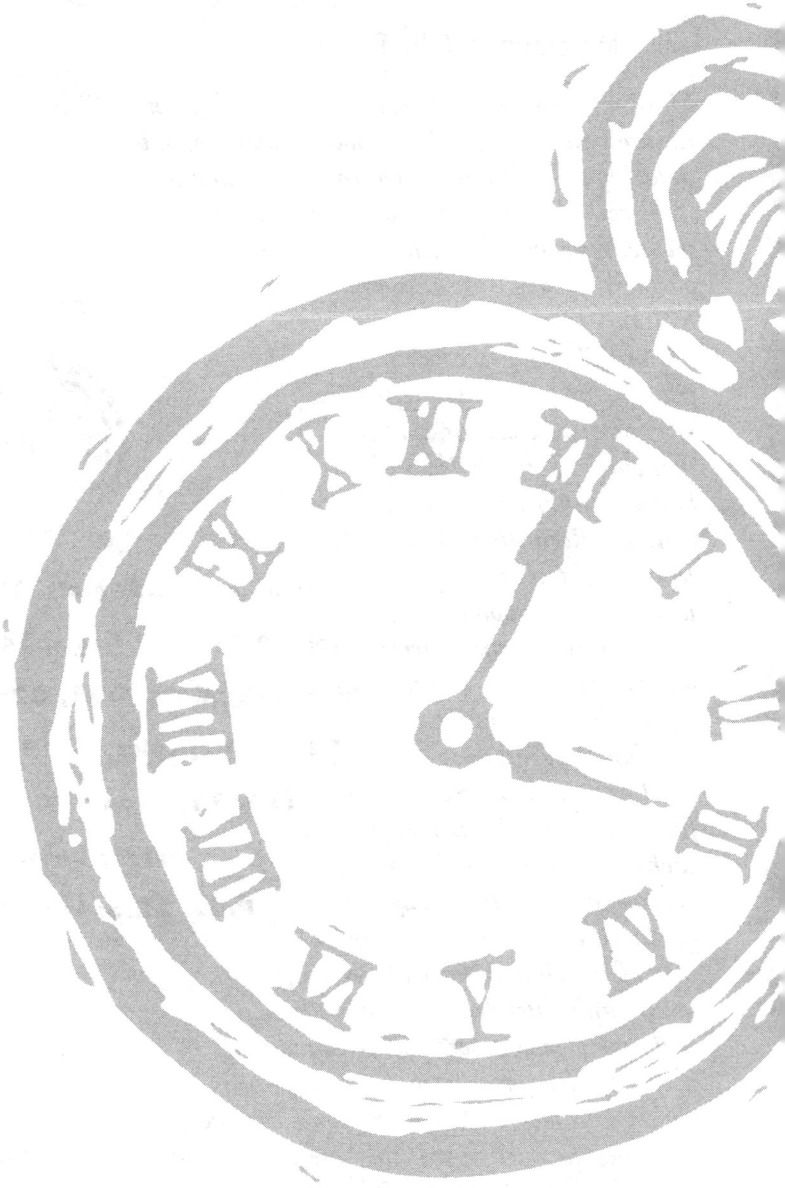

22 Marriage and the Family

Marriage was divinely established in Eden and affirmed by Jesus to be a lifelong union between a man and a woman in loving companionship. For the Christian a marriage commitment is to God as well as to the spouse, and should be entered into only by partners who share a common faith. Mutual love, honor, respect, and responsibility are the fabric of this relationship, which is to reflect the love, sanctity, closeness, and permanence of the relationship between Christ and His church. Regarding divorce, Jesus taught that the person who divorces a spouse, except for fornication, and marries another, commits adultery. Although some family relationships may fall short of the ideal, marriage partners who fully commit themselves to each other in Christ may achieve loving unity through the guidance of the Spirit and nurture of the church. God blesses the family and intends that its members shall assist each other toward complete maturity. Parents are to bring up their children to love and obey the Lord. By their example and their words they are to teach them that Christ is a loving disciplinarian, ever tender and caring, who wants them to become members of His body, the family of God. Increasing family closeness is one of the earmarks of the final gospel message.

Gen. 2:18-25; Matt. 19:3-9; John 2:1-11; 2 Cor. 6:14; Eph. 5:21-33; Matt. 5:31, 32; Mark 10:11, 12; Luke 16:18; 1 Cor. 7:10, 11; Exod. 20:12; Eph. 6:1-4; Deut. 6:5-9; Prov. 22:6; Mal. 4:5, 6.

Chapter 22

"How Is Mrs. Bruinsma? How Are the Children?"

It is interesting to note that the Adventist Church "believes" in marriage and in the family. And in this context the word "believes" is to be taken in its profound religious sense. We often say that we "believe" in certain things, just as a way of indicating our preference. But the people who composed and those who voted on our "Statement of Twenty-Seven Fundamental Beliefs" felt that marriage and the family have to do with our spiritual well-being—they are more than social conventions and are directly related to our religious convictions.

Having a "fundamental belief" that focuses on marriage and the family is in no way meant to discriminate against single people—those who have chosen to remain single or are single because of various circumstances, often beyond their control. Unfortunately, some of what is said and written in the church on this topic can be rather insensitive. At times I have participated in Sabbath School discussions on marriage and family values where single people must have felt utterly uncomfortable.

It struck me that this particular "fundamental belief" is one of the longest of all twenty-seven. It has just about as many words as number twenty-three, which deals with the heavenly sanctuary. Length is certainly not the only criterion to go by, but this in itself seems to reflect something of the importance we attach to this topic.

In many Western countries politicians have discovered that emphasizing family values will attract voters. The traditional nuclear family is under attack—or seems to be almost in the process of disappearing. In some countries, about half of all families now consist of people who live together and have children without having obtained an official marriage certificate; a large percentage of families have only one parent—often as the result of divorce but not infrequently by design. And families with two parents of the same gender are no longer the exceptions they once were.

But let's not kid ourselves. Even if we are critical of the kind of arrangements we just mentioned and compliment ourselves that we have stuck with the traditional pattern—father, mother, and (preferably two or three) children, we cannot automatically claim that all is well. The way many "regular" families operate in today's world is a far cry from what families ought to be. Many families in reality just consist of individuals who happen live in the same house, but each have their own programs and priorities. They may occasionally meet during a meal or at times watch TV in the same room but often spend very little quality time together. Basically they lead their own individual lives.

For a long time the Adventist community has pretended that, although there may be some problems in this area, on the whole the Adventist family functions much better than the average family. It has come as a shock to many of us that this is nothing but a myth. Admittedly, the divorce rates are still lower among Adventists than in society at large. But we are rapidly catching up, in particular, in the United States. (If there is one domain in church life where theory and practice are tragically divergent, it is in the area of divorce. I will not condemn people who, often after a long and terrible struggle, must conclude that their marriage does not work. But I continue to be amazed that the same people who routinely condemn church members in other countries because they wear a wedding ring will remain strangely silent when people divorce and remarry without paying much attention to the official view of the church in this matter.) And not only are divorce rates among Adventists on the rise, but in recent years enough research has been conducted to establish beyond any doubt that also in surprisingly many Adventist families wives are beaten and children are sexually and otherwise abused. Often these criminal offenses (for that is what they are) remain unreported; worse still, often the offenders continue to hold offices in the local church.

I guess, when I look at the Christian ideal for marriage and for family life as outlined in this fundamental belief, there are two sentiments that are firmly intermingled. I realize that I failed in many instances as a spouse and as a parent. I wish I could redo, or at least undo, certain things that I have done and said in the past. But on the other hand, I am extremely thankful that my family always has been, and is, loving and strong and supportive. We have lived on different continents, separated from each other by oceans and time zones, but we stayed remarkably close. In retrospect, the vast amounts we have paid for air travel and international telephone calls have been well spent!

Having now been married for some thirty-three years and having two children in their late twenties, I can only be thankful as I look back. We have been spared the disasters so many families have had to suffer: divorce, estrangement, educational and job failures, crime, and drugs. We have stayed close together as a family, even now as adults.

I realize that many people have not been as fortunate as I have been. And often I have wondered why some terrible things have happened to almost perfect families. If that realization should do anything, it should make me compassionate in my judgment when

I see how things sometimes go wrong (even when at times I feel I know why they did go wrong).

I am happy to see that attitude also prevailing in our church. More and more we have the courage to admit that many of the sins and troubles of society have also intruded into Adventist families; we are gradually facing up to the fact that we have serious cases of abuse within our ranks. We cannot hide the sad truth that many Adventist marriages sooner or later prove to be so irreparably damaged that divorce seems to be the only option that is left. Never should we simply accept this as a reality that cannot be changed. As a church, we must do all we can to keep the ideal clearly in focus. We must not hesitate to recognize trouble and deal with it when we see it. But we should be slow to give up on people and be, wherever possible, willing to give people the chance of a new beginning.

The other day I had a phone call from Africa. The principal of one of our schools wanted to ask me something. He did not come to the point straightaway but proceeded to ask about my family. How is Mrs. Bruinsma? How is your son? How is your daughter? As he went into quite a bit of detail, I began to be a little annoyed. I was busy. What did the man want? But then I remembered: That is what people in Africa do. For them family takes precedence over business. Come to think of it: As so often, they are right!

There is a sanctuary in heaven, the true tabernacle which the Lord set up and not man. In it Christ ministers on our behalf, making available to believers the benefits of His atoning sacrifice offered once and for all on the cross. He was inaugurated as our High Priest and began His intercessory ministry at the time of His ascension. In 1844, at the end of the prophetic period of 2300 days, He entered the second and last phase of His atoning ministry. It is a work of investigative judgment which is part of the ultimate disposition of all sin, typified by the cleansing of the ancient Hebrew sanctuary on the Day of Atonement. In that typical service the sanctuary was cleansed with the blood of animal sacrifices, but the heavenly things are purified with the perfect sacrifice of the blood of Jesus. The investigative judgment reveals to the heavenly intelligences who among the dead are asleep in Christ and therefore, in Him, are deemed worthy to have part in the first resurrection. It also makes manifest who, among the living are abiding in Christ, keeping the commandments of God and the faith of Jesus, and in Him, therefore, are ready for translation into his everlasting kingdom. This judgment vindicates the justice of God in saving those who believe in Jesus. It declares that those who have remained loyal to God shall receive the kingdom. The completion of this ministry of Christ will mark the end of human probation before the Second Advent.

Heb. 8:1-5; 4:14-16; 9:11-28; 10:19-22; 1:3; 2:16, 17; Dan. 7:9-27; 8:13, 14; 9:24-27; Num. 14:34; Ezek. 4:6; Lev. 16; Rev. 14:6, 7; 20:12; 14:12; 22:12.

Chapter 23

Bending Over Backward to Save Me!

My mother was, I am convinced, a pretty solid Seventh-day Adventist. She joined the church when she was about sixteen and remained a loyal and active member until she died at age seventy-nine. She did not have much formal education but was an intelligent woman with a more than average knowledge of the Scriptures. More than once she told me that the subject of the heavenly sanctuary bothered her. She would say: I try to understand how the 2300 days bring us to 1844, but I keep forgetting the details, and I would find it very hard to explain it to someone else. She often felt a bit embarrassed, even guilty, that as a longtime Adventist she had this problem with what had always been presented to her as a key doctrine. I repeatedly told her to relax about the arithmetic and focus on what it meant for her to have Christ as her High Priest, but I doubt whether I ever fully succeeded in convincing her.

To many Adventists, the ability to point to a particular year or even to a specific day seems to be the most comforting aspect of the doctrine of the heavenly sanctuary. This is something solid, something to hold on to. And, indeed, the reasoning that brings us from the beginning of the 2300 days of Daniel 8:14, in 457 B.C. to 1844 is quite compelling. The actual date—October 22—which is traditionally quoted as the exact time when Christ began the last phase of His high-priestly ministry, requires a few more assumptions, which most Adventists are probably unaware of. Recently, at the end of a meeting in London, a man approached me declaring that he had scientific proof that the October 22 date was an error. His research showed that the real date was October 21! He was extremely concerned that "the brethren" were conspiring to keep this precious truth from the church members. I am afraid I cannot get very excited about whether October 22 or October 21 is the correct day. But I can get excited about knowing that earth's history is in its final phase and that preparations are under way for the grand finale, when Christ will come and will claim His own!

I do not want to get sucked into any debate about whether there is a real building with two "apartments" in heaven. Personally, I do not think that the language of the Bible requires us to believe that. We are dealing with heavenly realities but must be content with human metaphors and symbols. What I believe these metaphors and symbols tell us is that the process of putting things right between God and man reaches beyond the Cross. Today, as you read these lines, Christ is still involved in getting us to our final destination. A pre-Advent judgment, or whatever you want to call it, has been going on for a considerable time and will soon conclude its business. Or, in words that we humans can understand: The final list of those who will share eternity with their Lord is presently being composed.

There are lots of questions we must leave unanswered. For instance: How is this pre-Advent judgment organized? And does the Lord really need more than one hundred and fifty years to work all of this out? It would be interesting to know some of these things, but what difference does it really make? The one most important point is that Christ is my High Priest. He continues to be personally involved in my ultimate destiny.

To many, the very idea of judgment brings fear. What if this heavenly tribunal concludes that I am not good enough for the kingdom? What a terrifying thought that all my sins, from my early childhood until today, are being revisited. There are so many things I am ashamed of, so many mistakes I wish would remain buried rather than being rehashed.

Indeed, I would have every reason for panic if I were judged by my peers, by my colleagues, or any terrestrial jury. But that is precisely the point: The one and only judgment that finally matters is not on earth but in heaven. And Jesus Christ is the Judge. All I know about Him should put my misgivings to rest. Christ is not trying to keep people out of the kingdom. He is doing all He can to bring as many in as He possibly can. He bends over backward to save me. Only my utter stupidity and stubbornness can cause me to be lost. My case is in His hands. If I can just remember this for the rest of my life, I have nothing to worry about. He is personally involved with my case. It does not get buried in any heavenly bureaucracy.

So, what does the doctrine of the heavenly sanctuary do for me? Does it give me an uneasy feeling, as I wonder whether I will come through? Quite the contrary: If ever there is a truth that sets me free, it is this glorious realization that Christ has taken a personal interest in my case and that He is the kind of Person who will make sure that I will not be forgotten when He comes to round up the citizens of His new world.

24 The Second Coming of Christ

The second coming of Christ is the blessed hope of the church, the grand climax of the gospel. The Saviour's coming will be literal, personal, visible, and worldwide. When He returns, the righteous dead will be resurrected, and together with the righteous living will be glorified and taken to heaven, but the unrighteous will die. The almost complete fulfillment of most lines of prophecy, together with the present condition of the world, indicates that Christ's coming is imminent. The time of the event has not been revealed, and we are therefore exhorted to be ready at all times.

Titus 2:13; Heb. 9:28;

John 14:1-3; Acts 1:9-11;

Matt. 24:14; Rev. 1:7;

Matt. 24:43, 44;

1 Thess. 4:13-18;

1 Cor. 15:51-54;

2 Thess. 1:7-10; 2:8;

Rev. 14:14-20; 19:11-21;

Matt. 24; Mark 13; Luke 21;

2 Tim. 3:1-5; 1 Thess. 5:1-6.

Chapter 24

Trusting in the One Who Is Coming

From my childhood onward I have been exposed to sermons about the soon coming of Christ. (And yes, I suppose, those church members who complain that in the past there were more sermons on that topic, have a point!) I remember how in my childish fantasies I imagined how Christ would suddenly arrive and how—together with my parents, my little brother and my sisters, with our belongings in the two old suitcases we always used to take when we went to stay with our grandparents—I would begin the journey to heaven on a big cloud, surrounded by other families on other clouds! As I became older such notions were exchanged for somewhat less fanciful ideas, but the theme of Christ's soon coming continued to occupy much of my thinking. Instead of being excited about the nearness of His coming, I began to be concerned. I secretly hoped that He would not make too much haste. That was especially true as I grew into adolescence and early adulthood. I was worried that I would not have time to get married and that I would not be able to enjoy the many good things of life. In fact, I thought it would be best if He came when I would be about seventy years old. That would give me the best of both worlds: I would enjoy a full life here without having to die eventually!

Gradually it began to dawn on me that this kind of egocentric thinking can hardly be called Christian. I came to realize that, having been born in the Western world, my chances of having a pleasant life were rather good. And also, that the vast majority of people in this world are less fortunate: Those who have been born in the shanty towns of Calcutta, Kinshasa, and Mexico City have fewer positive things to look forward to. Should the homeless people in Bangladesh and the victims of famine and drought in Africa have to wait a little longer for the final solution to their problems, just so I can have extra time to enjoy life?

Through the years I have struggled with this hesitancy on my part to welcome the idea of Christ's return with enthusiasm. But I have come to realize that this secret hope that Christ would postpone His coming a little longer is due to a serious misunderstanding. It is based on the mistaken idea that life here is in competition with the life hereafter; that eternal life is a threat to our present existence: If Christ were to come tomorrow, we would miss so many interesting and beautiful things! I am beginning to understand that we must not play the present life off against the life of the future, as if the future life destroys the value and the enjoyment of our present existence. Life here can be an abundant life (John 10:10), even though for many it also brings much misery and suffering. Life in the future is guaranteed to be abundant beyond our finite imagination.

Something else has troubled me for many years. In the few decades since my childhood the sermons I have listened to have tried to convince me that "the signs of the end" are clearer than ever. In actual fact, to me the reverse sometimes seemed to be true. As the years passed I could muster less and less excitement when I heard or read about the Lisbon earthquake of 1755 and the dark day of 1780 and the falling of the stars in 1833. This all seemed so long ago! And it seemed that the frequent earthquakes and famines, and the wars in different parts of the globe, were just more of the same thing.

Of course, there were the sermons about the dramatic increase in power of the Roman Catholic Church. But seeing the developments of Catholicism in Western Europe, I could only conclude that whatever changes there had been in Catholicism, they had been for the better and not for the worse! Whatever interest the charts of last-day-events may have held for me in the past, this has slowly but surely evaporated. I sensed that any detailed timetable of last-day events, with a clear chronological order of the last seven plagues, the Sunday laws and "the death decree," the sifting and the time of trouble, etc. was a far too human approach to "the last things."

I am not for a minute suggesting that these topics should not be studied and that we should not pause to think about the seriousness and finality of the "final events." But we should always realize that we only know in part and that many Bible texts underline the suddenness and total unexpectedness of the Second Coming. In fact, I am convinced that these complicated charts are the result of a persistent refusal to accept that we do not know the day or the hour! I am afraid some people get so obsessed by there ingenious chronologies and schemes that Christ is in danger of being eclipsed from their study of events leading up to His return.

The time of the end is repeatedly compared with the days of Noah. Could it be, I wonder, that we should pay more attention to that one great divine "sign" that God gave after the Flood was over: the rainbow that so often appears in the sky to tell us of God's commitment to see mankind through?

Could it be that the many "signs of the times" that have occurred ever since Christ's first coming, but have increased in intensity and frequency, are constant signals along the road to the kingdom, telling us you are not forgotten? History moves slowly but surely to its final goal.

In recent years we have seen several books about the apparent delay of Christ's second coming. We seem to be embarrassed by the fact that "it takes so long." We have been preaching the advent message for well over one hundred and fifty years! What has gone wrong? How human can we be? How pretentious it is to think that God's time schedule must somehow coincide with our corporate sense of timing. Recently I read the remarks of a Messianic Jew who believed in the future conversion of the people of Israel. In response to a question whether nineteen centuries of waiting had not dampened his hopes, he exclaimed. "Nineteen centuries?" Even if it takes another nineteen centuries, or even one hundred centuries: it will happen!" I do not believe it will take another nineteen centuries before Christ will come. But even if it would take another century or so, that in no way invalidates the advent hope!

In his book *Now and Not Yet* (Review and Herald Publishing Association, 1987), John Brunt asks the question why our hope for the return of Christ is often rather tepid. His words seemed to have been written for me personally. "First," he says, "we are not completely sure about the One who is coming. We are not sure we can trust Him. His justice seems so severe." Our relationship with Him is not so intimate that we trust Him implicitly and would want nothing more intensely than that He would come today. "Secondly, we are unsure about our own preparation. Maybe God will find one defect of character." Maybe we are not good enough to be accepted by Him. This worry is the logical sequel of our first problem, that we do not know the Lord as we should. If we really knew Him, we would be absolutely sure that His provisions for our deficiencies are more than adequate. "Finally," Brunt continues, "too often we focus our attention on the events that occur before the Second Coming instead of on the One who comes and on the new Kingdom He has prepared for us."

Something to think about, isn't it?

25 Death and Resurrection

The wages of sin is death. But God, who alone is immortal, will grant eternal life to His redeemed. Until that day death is an unconscious state for all people. When Christ, who is our life, appears, the resurrected righteous and the living righteous will be glorified and caught up to meet their Lord. The second resurrection, of the unrighteous, will take place a thousand years later.

Rom. 6:23; 1 Tim. 6:15, 16;

Eccl. 9:5, 6; Ps. 146:3, 4;

John 11:11-14; Col. 3:4;

1 Cor. 15:51-54;

1 Thess. 4:13-17;

John 5:28, 29;

Rev. 20:1-10.

Chapter 25

Safe (Saved) in God's Mercy

I have no idea whether I am "abnormal" or "atypical" in my attitude toward death. I do not think I am obsessed by my own mortality yet there are few days when I do not give it at least a cursory thought: Sooner or later I am going to die. My father died at the age of fifty. It gives me a funny feeling to realize that I have already beaten him when it comes to survival. My mother died when she was seventy-nine. If heredity has anything to do with it, I may possibly count on reaching at least the age of about sixty-five, the average life-span of my two parents. But come to think of it, that is only about ten years from the moment I am writing these lines. Maybe I should get some comfort from the thought that my grandparents on both sides lived fairly long lives! However, that did not seem to help my brother who died when he was only eight or my sister who passed away in her early thirties as a result of a brain tumor. All this is, of course, useless speculation. But of one thing I can be pretty sure: At age fifty-five, more than 50 percent of my life is behind me. Chances are rather slim that I will reach 110!

I pray God for a long and healthy life. My life is not perfect, but I really have not too much to complain about. I do not think that death truly frightens me, but I am certainly not looking forward to it. I enjoy life, and I hope to continue to enjoy it, together with my wife and—from some distance—my two children. Death would be unwelcome! As a Christian I have no qualms about stating this.

After all, the Bible refers to death as an enemy (1 Corinthians 15:26)! Death often is preceded by illness and pain. And I must admit, I am not good in dealing with illness and pain. Death causes sorrow. If I were to die before my wife (statistics indicate that this is quite likely) and before my children (I fervently hope that to be the case), it will cause deep anxiety to those who are dearest to me. I have no doubt that they love me enough to be brokenhearted if suddenly I were no longer with them. And I simply would not know how to cope if I were to know that I was not going to precede them in death.

Adventists believe we will remain in a state of unconsciousness until the resurrection. I have no idea what that means. The Bible does not give any detailed information. It uses the metaphors of "sleep," of "being naked," of "dust turning to dust." Other Christians believe they have an immortal something—a soul—that leaves their body and ascends to heaven. More and more it is recognized that this idea has no basis in Scripture but is derived from Greek philosophy. Death simply is the end of our earthly existence. That is all we know.

But if that were the end of the story, I would feel rather empty. Fifty, sixty, seventy, perhaps eighty or ninety years—followed by total nothingness. If that were all there is, my life would in actual fact be like that of any animal: birth-growth-deterioration-nothingness. But nothing could be farther from the truth than this.

Somehow my existence does not end at death. There is life after death. Not the kind of life we now experience—tainted with death from the moment we are born. Rather, a new kind of life, eternal life. More than just lasting longer, it will have a different quality. Every moment will be quality time. There will never be a moment when I will be bored, because I do not know what to do with my time; nor will I ever again feel frustrated by a lack of time. It is indeed hard to imagine what that will be like.

Although all my anxiety about death and dying is not taken away, it makes a crucial difference to know that death is not the final word. There is a future. I am not written off when I have ceased to be an active citizen and can no longer contribute to society. After a short intermezzo I will have a new lease on life—eternal life.

How can I be sure that I will not be forgotten when God brings the dead back to life? The Bible tells us not to worry: Our names are written in His "book of life." When He hands out this eternal life, He will come to the letter B, and toward the end of that rubric, He will find Bruinsma, Reinder (1942-?). Of course, this "book of life" is just a metaphor to underline that God has His administration in order. If John had been writing today, he would probably have said that our names are all in God's supercomputer. When He does His final printout, God's children will all be on the list!

All of us are unique. It is a uniqueness that goes far beyond our DNA. God keeps track of this uniqueness of each of his creatures. He knows what makes me this absolutely unique being that I am. And somehow He preserves the record. Sooner or (I hope) later I will die. The atoms which now constitute my body will become part of something else. I will live on in the memory of those who love me. But that memory will fade as time goes on. And that memory will, no doubt, be quite selective. I will, however, live on in God's memory as the unique, one-of-a-kind creature that He loves and will not allow to disappear. I am safe (or should I say saved?) in His memory.

Knowing this makes all the difference. Because, in a very real sense, this life now becomes the prelude to eternal life. There may still be lots of questions about all the bad things that happen to good people, but I can trust God that somehow in His eternal perspective things make sense, and that very soon He will make it up to all of us. And it surely also impacts on the way I look at people around me. They also are candidates for this new, unending life. And if they don't know about that, I had better tell them!

Again: The idea of death and dying still makes me uncomfortable. But it makes a real difference to know that death is not total oblivion, but a temporary stop on the way of life. At the end of the dark tunnel of death the light of God's love will await me. And that is really all I need to know.

26 The Millennium and the End of Sin

The millennium is the thousand-year reign of Christ with His saints in heaven between the first and the second resurrections. During this time the wicked dead will be judged; the earth will be utterly desolate, without living human inhabitants, but occupied by Satan and his angels. At its close Christ with His saints and the Holy City will descend from heaven to earth. The unrighteous dead will then be resurrected, and with Satan and his angels will surround the city; but fire from God will consume them and cleanse the earth. The universe will thus be freed of sin and sinners forever.

Rev. 20; 1 Cor. 6:2, 3; Jer. 4:23-26; Rev. 21:1-5; Mal. 4:1; Ezek. 28:18, 19.

Chapter 26

A Call to Mission

There is only one chapter in the Bible that directly deals with the millennium (the period of one thousand years). Yet, few subjects have received so much attention from Christian writers in past and present as this. In evangelical circles the millennium is still a hotly debated topic. You are either a premillennialist of some sort or belong to the postmillennialist school. Premillennialists believe that Christ returns to this earth before this period of one thousand years begins, while postmillennialists contend that the millennium will precede the Second Coming. And then there are the amillennialists, who reject both theories and believe that the one thousand years is symbolic rather than literal and spans the era of the church, between Christ's stay on earth some twenty centuries ago and His Second Coming.

This description of the various approaches to the millennium does not do any justice to the multitude of variations in these main themes. Elements that invariably enter into the discussion are the "secret rapture" and the "tribulation!"

Adventists are solid premillennialists. They firmly believe that the period of one thousand years follows the Second Coming of Christ. They also have very definite beliefs about what happens at the beginning, during, and at the end of the millennium.

Explanations usually are accompanied by a scheme that outlines the main points. When Christ comes, the righteous dead are raised and the living righteous receive immortality. The unbelievers of all ages, including those who are alive at the moment of the Second Coming, will die and/or remain dead during the thousand years. They will be resurrected at the end of the millennium and will face the second death.

During the thousand years the earth will be empty. Satan will be incapacitated, for there is no one he can deceive, while the "saints" (those who were resurrected or immortalized) have a role in the divine judgment. They are in heaven awaiting their inheritance: the new earth.

Are you still with me? I wonder how many felt the temptation to simply skip this long explanation. It sounds so unreal, so schematic. Some may say: It is interesting to know these things. But really, what does this tell us? OK, somehow we will have a role in God's judgment. But it remains difficult to imagine what that will be like. And why in the world does God need one thousand years? Surely, If He is omniscient, He can work a bit faster than that. Or is this number 1,000 not to be taken literally? And why would there be a resurrection of the "unrighteous" dead of all times if soon thereafter they are going to be executed in the second death?

Through the years I have wondered: Is this useful information? How does this help me in my faith? Why does God want me to know these things? And if He wanted us to be informed, could He not have achieved this in a more lucid way that would not have given rise to so many conflicting theories? These questions have not gone away. And yet, more recently I have begun to attach greater value to Revelation 20. Let me explain.

The idea that all people will eventually be saved is not new. Many have argued that God is love and that this in itself would be guarantee that He would redeem everyone. Does not Scripture say that God does not want anyone "to perish" (2 Peter 3:9)? And surely, what God wants is going to happen! Today we hear many voices from all corners of Christendom that echo the same sentiment. It may be a long process, but ultimately God will save the world, not one person excepted. That sounds very attractive. If true, this idea has many implications. One is that missionary work in whatever shape or form is totally unnecessary. Whether people are reached with the gospel message and respond to it does not matter: They will be saved anyway!

Revelation 20 paints a completely different picture. The destiny of those who are on God's side is diametrically opposed to that of those who are on the other side. For the first category there is life, first during the millennium (whatever kind of life that may be) and then unto all eternity. For the others there is only judgment and eternal death. All of this leaves many questions. But Revelation 20 in the most forceful way possible underlines what many other Bible passages teach: There is not one, but there are two destinations. And our eternal destination depends on the deliberate choice we make: accepting Christ as our Lord or rejecting Him.

If so much is at stake, surely we must do all we can to get that message out. People have to be told about Christ; they must be urged to accept Him and follow Him. I, as one of the followers of Christ, cannot stand aloof but must do what I can to tell others about Christ and the abundant life, here and beyond, that is there for the asking.

Looking at Revelation 20 and its message of the millennium from this angle has helped me greatly to appreciate this chapter. Reading it, I no longer have the immediate mental image of a time line, with events indicated at the beginning, during, and at the end of the 1,000 year period. For me the overarching impact of the chapter has become its implied call to mission, to the church corporately, and to me individually. If so much is at stake for those around me and for those far away, I simply cannot remain inactive!

27 The New Earth

On the new earth, in which righteousness dwells, God will provide an eternal home for the redeemed and a perfect environment for everlasting life, love, joy, and learning in His presence. For here God Himself will dwell with His people, and suffering and death will have passed away. The great controversy will be ended, and sin will be no more. All things, animate and inanimate, will declare that God is love; and He shall reign forever. Amen.

2 Peter 3:13;

Isa. 35; 65:17-25;

Matt. 5:5; Rev. 21:1-7;

22:1-5; 11:15.

Chapter 27

When Life Cannot Be Better

Some months ago I saw a book with an intriguing title that I could not resist buying. I was not disappointed when I read it. In *The History of Heaven* (New Haven, 1990), Colleen McDannell and Bernhard Lang relate how, through the centuries, the ideas of what heaven will be like have fluctuated and changed as circumstances differed and cultures and societies have changed. The book provides a fascinating account of how these changes in the way heaven was perceived were not only reflected in theological and other religious writings but also in the fine arts. And indeed, one does not have to visit too many museums to establish that medieval pictures of the hereafter differ greatly from modern pictorial impressions of heaven!

We know very little about what heaven and the new earth will be like. In fact, we have been more fully informed about what will not be there than about what will be. Certain categories of people are excluded: Those who have intentionally, deliberately, unrepentantly aligned themselves with the evil forces of spiritual Babylon will not be able to enter the New Jerusalem. Sin will not be there, nor the consequences of sin! That will make all the difference: no more dying and death; no more tears; no more AIDS or Alzheimer's disease. There will be no more funerals or hospitals; no more doctors or nurses or psychiatrists. No more loneliness, no more deceit, no more lies.

It is hard to imagine what a world without all these horrible things will be like. But we have at least some faint idea of what this means. These unpleasant, often heart-rending, experiences will have come to an end. The new world order will not have Tutsis and Hutus murdering each other nor Catholics and Protestants hating each other nor Whites discriminating against Blacks nor men dominating women.

But what more can we say?

John the Revelator did his very best when he tried to put in words what he was shown in his visions. He saw a city. In some ways it looked like the kind of city he knew: a place with high walls and strong gates. I have no doubt that he used symbolic language. How else are we to make sense of his descriptions? His new Jerusalem has streets of gold. It has the shape of a cube and rises to a height of some 2,000 miles. I believe these symbolic descriptions have a deep meaning. (To give an example: You remember another place that had the form of a cube? Yes, it was the holy of holies in the Old Testament sanctuary, where God was present in a very special way. Could it be that by describing Jerusalem as a cube, John wanted to emphasize the ultimate presence of God with his people?) This, however, is not the place to explore the precise meaning of all the symbols John used to evoke in our minds as visual images of the new city of God.

But just as John could only try to express the reality of the coming new world order in terms and pictures of his days, others' understanding of what he wrote has through the ages contributed to "the history of heaven." And that is the only way in which you and I can get some insight into the new world awaiting us. To me it seems that the key to our sanctified imaginations is found in Revelation 21:5, where John quotes the divine promise: "I am making everything new." Note, the promise is not that God will make all kinds of new things but rather that He will make all things new! The Greek word in the original text refers to a newness in quality. Everything is remade to a level of perfection that is beyond our wildest dreams. Does that not give us the right to do some extrapolating on the basis of some of our most precious experiences in our present life?

In the past few years I have attended several leadership seminars. Each time I have been told about the importance of "visioning." The instructor would ask the participants to focus their thoughts on the most pleasant place we had ever been to. My mind would almost immediately turn to a stretch of beach some twenty-five miles east of the West-African city of Abidjan. During the years my wife and I lived in Ivory Coast, we would often on Sunday mornings relax under the palm trees on that beautiful stretch of tropical beach. We would sometimes get tired of the vendors who would try to sell us their fake Rolex watches and imitation LaCoste shirts, but we would never get tired of the sight and sound of the ocean. We often think with nostalgia of the many hours spent around the picnic table together with friends, about all the delicious meals we had and the countless games of Scrabble we played (either in Dutch, French, or English). Well, heaven to me is like that, but then, of course, much better, unimaginably more perfect!

Jesus once made a remark that has worried many Bible readers ever since. In a discussion with a group of religious leaders He was asked a hypothetical question about heaven. His discussion partners wanted to drive Him into a corner and pressed Him to tell them what would happen to someone who had been married seven times. To which of the seven men would this woman be married in heaven? Jesus did not fall into the trap. He told them that in heaven things will function on a different level. Does that mean that there will be no longer any difference between the genders? From my present perspective I would find that a rather unhappy prospect.

But if it is true that God is going to renew all things, it must also include a renewal of all human relationships. That would give me the right to search my memory and replay the best moments I ever had with others—with my spouse, with my children, with relatives and friends. Fortunately, I have had many precious moments when I felt close to others, to loved ones, and to friends. But, unfortunately, these moments have often alternated with moments of misunderstanding and tension. That situation will be radically different in the new world. Our most precious experiences with others in this world are but a faint reflection of how we will then relate to others. Whatever friendship and love we have known here will be ours, but without any of the negative experiences, and on a unimaginably higher level.

There are other dimensions we might add. I am in reasonably good health (I think) as I write these lines. But I have just had ten physiotherapy sessions to relieve some of the stiffness in my neck and shoulders. As I wrote the previous paragraphs I succumbed to the temptation to eat a bar of chocolate, although I know that I need to lose at least fifteen pounds. I know I would feel fitter if I would get more physical exercise and would be more careful in how much I eat. I admit that I often feel tired, even exhausted, after a busy week and, to the distress of my wife, cannot keep my eyes open on Sabbath afternoon. But once in a while there are moments that I feel really great—at the end of a good vacation or when spring arrives and we can sit in the garden for the first time after a long winter. That's the kind of life I wish I would feel in my bones every day of the week. Well, heaven will provide that kind of life, constantly, eternally, but on a much more elevated level than I have ever experienced.

I could add some other aspects. But this, I believe, makes the point. God allows me to write my own postscript in the history of heaven. Whatever is good in my life here, it will be there—only much better!